Real Fast Desserts

ALSO BY NIGEL SLATER

Real Fast Food
The marie claire Cookbook
Real Good Food
The 30-Minute Cook

NIGEL SLATER

Real Fast Desserts

OVER 200 DESSERTS AND SWEET SNACKS IN 30 MINUTES

THE OVERLOOK PRESS

WOODSTOCK • NEW YORK

First published in the United States in 1997 by
The Overlook Press
Lewis Hollow Road
Woodstock, New York 12498

Copyright © 1997 Nigel Slater
Illustrations © Val Archer

Library of Congress Cataloging-in-Publications Data

Slater, Nigel.
Real fast desserts / Nigel Slater.
p. cm.
1. Quick and easy cookery. 2. Desserts. I. Title
TX833.5.S5897   1997   641.8'6—dc20   96-29312

TYPE FORMATTING BY BERNARD SCHLEIFER

Printed in the United States of America
First Edition
10 9 8 7 6 5 4 3 2 1

Contents

INTRODUCTION

This is not a book of instant indulgences. *Real Fast Desserts* is simply a collection of ways in which you might like to end your meal, most of which take very little time to prepare. Some are literally instant (it takes just seconds to drop a few velvety raspberries into a glass of chilled Gewürztraminer), while others take a full half hour. This book aims to do nothing more than show you what wonderful ways there are to finish a meal, some of which you might not have thought of.

I believe passionately that everyone should allow themselves just an hour a day in which to make themselves something good to eat. If they can share what they make with someone, then even better. But it is not always realistic to ask even that, which is why there were some ten-minute main courses in my last book, and even more ten-minute desserts in this one.

I find it more and more difficult to finish my meals on a savory note. I will happily eat a piece of cheese to finish off the wine, but a morsel of something sweet, perhaps just a mouthful of vanilla ice cream and a liquor-soaked prune or a crisp water biscuit topped with tart berries and sweet whipped cream, is nigh on essential. I am not alone. Almost every letter I received after the publication of *Real Fast Food*, to which this is the companion volume, suggested that I had successfully enticed people back into the kitchen only to abandon them when it came to the dessert stage. This book is not a guide to tarting up instant puddings from a package or "a hundred ways with frozen waffles." Neither will it let you get away with custard powder or canned frosting. The whole point of setting down the hundred, no, two hundred, or so ideas is to show that real food, by which I mean fresh food simply prepared at home with love, need not stop with the main course just because time is not on your side. And when is it?

Imagine a fig bulging with ripe scarlet seeds or a slice of per-fect, luscious pear with a piece of grainy Parmesan cheese, or perhaps a thin, crisp apple toast hot from the oven. Consider blackberries steeped in a glass of rich red Barolo or a dish of

7

creamy rice scented with rosewater and pistachios. All these are fast desserts. All of them are light years away from the instant puddings in packages or cans. And most take less of your time than the average store-bought dessert takes to reheat or a frozen cheesecake takes to thaw.

Friends always expect a dessert when they come over for supper. On the occasions I have ended the meal with cheese there have been looks of barely concealed disappointment that I haven't produced a dish of boozy trifle or even a crêpe with sugar and lemon. Many of the recipes here will prove suitable for entertaining, though most are meant to liven up the daily meal.

I have no time for those spoilsports who suggest that desserts are unhealthy. Of course, any form of over-indulgent eating is unacceptable nowadays, but you will find no suggestion in these pages that a rib-sticking bread pudding or a creamy dessert should be an everyday affair. It should be noted that the backbone of the book is fruit. I find it difficult to think of a day in which fruit in some form is not consumed in my house. In summer it may be berries squashed and stirred into yogurt as a quick form of fool, or in winter an almond-topped crisp. Here you will find fruit in abundance: roasted, grilled, puréed, baked, and brûléed. And I make no apologies for it.

Many of the suggestions are simply classics with their corners cut—a bread pudding made with fruity, buttery *panettone* rather than laboriously buttered white bread, a summer pudding made without the traditional overnight wait, or a *tiramisu* that seems none the worse from forgoing its usual chilling time. Whatever quick ways you use, the most important considerations are flavor and pleasure.

A Few Points

Ripeness

I go on about ripeness all the time. It will probably drive you quite mad. But in fruits, as in cheese or game, ripeness is all. The difference between a fragrant, meltingly soft pear that dribbles juice down your chin and a hard, grainy pear is that one is begging you to eat it, the other not. A truly ripe mango is a gift from heaven, as is a plate of pineapple slices caught just in time, though both are ludicrously juicy to eat. An unripe apple will keep its aromatic subtlety all to itself, apart from giving you a stomachache.

The point at which fruit is ready can be subjective, though generally I insist that nothing is ready unless you can smell it from six inches away. An underripe melon is not worth eating, yet I prefer a slightly firm banana, and an underripe blackberry will still have the welcome trace of acidity now lost in the cultivated ones. But for me, much of the point in eating fruit of any kind is its juice. The more fragrant and sweet the better. It's what makes fruit sexy.

Choosing fruit at its best takes a little care, and I have offered as many clues as I can throughout the book to guide you to picking out the best. Better one fat fig at its brief moment of perfect ripeness than a hundred slices of devil's food cake.

"I Don't Have Time to Make Desserts"

You don't need half an hour to scatter a few fresh basil leaves over a bowl of strawberries. And it takes barely five minutes to slice a ripe pineapple and sprinkle it with Kirsch. Pan-fried apples with *crème fraîche* can be yours in ten minutes, while even banana custard made with proper egg custard takes little more than fifteen. So don't talk such nonsense.

"I Can't Afford to Make Desserts"

I feel very strongly about this one. No matter how hard the stores try to keep prices down, and no matter how carefully I shop, I never cease to be amazed at the bill at the checkout.

I do not have a fortune to spend on food, though I will admit things are getting better. I have deliberately avoided expensive ingredients, unnecessary lavishness, or wastefulness. But not at the expense of flavor. There are no more than a handful of expensive recipes in the book, unless, that is, you buy your raspberries out of season and in a chic market. But that is another matter.

REAL FAST FOOD

Real Fast Food is a collection of some 350 ideas for things to cook when you are in a hurry to eat. It was the book that spawned *Real Fast Desserts*, so if you don't have a copy then I suggest you go out and buy one as this second book will then make much more sense. And I will have sold another book.

SPEEDING UP YOUR COOKING

I have written on this at length in the above, but there are one or two points that are particularly pertinent to desserts.

I am a great believer in cutting corners. Who wants their daily cooking to resemble an exam at cooking school? Not that I would ever put cooking schools down; I think they are wonderful things. I just don't want to run my life like one.

I assume that you have bought this book simply because you want to make your family, your friends, or yourself something nice to eat when you get home, but have very little time or inclination to do so. I will not assume that you want to run around whirling-dervish-style at six o'clock at night. The style here is laid back, to say the least. You will find that most of the recipes offer much flavor for exceedingly little work. That is the whole point of the book.

PLANNING AND PRECOOKING

You won't find much of that in here. I have avoided suggesting you marinate the lemon zest in the brandy before you leave for work in the morning, superwoman fashion. I know the state I am in when I leave for work in the morning. Marinating lemon zest is not on my agenda. At 8 o'clock in the morning I can't even make the bed, let alone grate a lemon.

Neither will I assume you have a freezer big enough to freeze a side of beef. Or that you are the sort of person who has the time or inclination to have fanatically labeled prebaked tart shells in the freezer. I don't actually have one, unless you count the box at the top of the refrigerator; and that is packed full with just one bag of coffee beans, a carton of vanilla ice cream, and a couple of slabs of puff pastry. There are also a couple of ice-cube trays that smell ever-so-slightly of the cats' fish that was once in there, and badly need replacing. And that is when it hasn't frozen up to the point when I could barely post a letter through it.

CALORIES

Many people are concerned about their calorie intake, and often tend to avoid eating desserts as a result. I have found that almost anything marked "low in calories" also means "low in flavor." It seems sad that this should be the case, but it is. For my money, I would rather eat two spoonfuls of something truly delicious but high in calories and fat, say mascarpone cheese with apricot and almonds, than an entire low-calorie, lowfat cheesecake. That said, I have included hundreds of suggestions for desserts that contain very few of the dreaded things at all and that will fit neatly into any diet where calories are being counted. However, I remain convinced that a combination of more exercise and smaller portions of delicious food is probably better for you in the long run than getting het up and stressed-out every time you feel like a scoop of ice cream.

SUGAR

I use sugar in this book. With one or two exceptions I only use sugar where it actually improves the flavor of something. The exceptions generally concern texture or quite simply making something work. I would like to say that strawberries are better without a minute sprinkling of sugar, but they rarely are, or that a little of the deadly white stuff is not really necessary on a crêpe, but it is.

For the most part I use unrefined granulated sugar, though I still use the refined white stuff from time to time, especially if I am making caramel. (Tricky stuff, caramel.) Artificial sweeteners are quite disgusting, leaving an aftertaste in the mouth that only the palate-dead cannot detect. Honey is not always a suitable substitute, and I find brown sugars have a bullying, pervasive flavor that is rarely complementary to the recipe. You can take it, though, that if it has been possible to leave sugar out then I have, but where the battle has been between not using sugar and losing flavor then I am afraid flavor has won.

BUTTER AND MARGARINE

It is butter every time. I will not have margarine in my house. Anything made with margarine leaves a greasy coating on the roof of one's mouth, akin to a mouthful of Vaseline. No, sorry, it has to be butter. And when I say butter, you can take it that I mean unsalted.

CREAM

I use light and heavy whipping cream and *crème fraîche* in some of the recipes and suggest them as accompaniments to several of the dishes. I am aware that many people are concerned about their intake of dairy products, particularly of the high fat ones such as heavy creams. As I have said before, I am not advocating a cream-rich dessert every night, and like most things I suppose that that boring old maxim "in moderation" must apply here too. I could also point out, though, that the French have one of the lowest rates of heart attacks in the world. And we all know how they like their dairy products.

The finest quality cream is creamy-yellow in color and has a slight acidity. It has a wonderfully rich flavor and is almost without exception the product of smaller dairies. In much the same way that people who have been brought up on wooly, insipid, mass–produced chicken find free-range birds a bit "gamey" (all chicken *used* to taste that way), those who have tasted only thin, sterilized creams may actually think real cream tastes slightly "off."

If possible, avoid any cream marked "ultra-pasteurized." This is cream which has undergone pasteurization at very high temperature, designed to give it a longer shelf-life. Cream that has suffered this process will have a somewhat "cooked" flavor, and is hard to whip.

Light table or coffee cream, which contains too little butterfat to allow it to thicken when whipped, is fine for accompanying fruit salads and in coffee, though I have to say I rarely use it.

Light and heavy whipping creams are the ones suitable for most cooking. They are also the ones for whipping. It is easier to overwhip cream than to get it right. Whipped cream should be thick enough to form drifts, but not so stiff that it will stand in peaks. If it looks yellow and grainy then it has gone too far. The trick with whipping cream is to use chilled cream and a cold, dry bowl. The mixing bowl that you have rinsed in hot water and shaken dry will almost certainly help your cream to curdle. If using an electric mixer use a medium speed. The fast one is difficult to control, especially as the cream thickens, and if you use the slow setting you will be there all night. As a general rule, stop just before you think it is thick enough, then finish the job with a hand balloon whisk or rotary beater. It's one more thing to wash up, but better than a bowlful of butter.

Crème fraîche Wonderful stuff. A peculiarly rich cream, popular in France, it is now gaining ground over here. The joy of the thick, spoonable yellow cream is its slight piquancy, which stops it from cloying, and its absurdly rich texture.

Clotted cream I rather like clotted cream, thick, rich, and yellow underneath a thin, slightly crisp skin. Most of it comes from Devon and Cornwall, in England, and is sold in cute wax cartons or little plastic pots. Known internationally as *the* accompaniment to scones and jam, a spoonful is quite sublime with fruit tarts or eaten off the same spoon as a juicy prune. It is sad that it has gone out of fashion, even in England. You can blame the calorie counters for that. No one should have told them it contains almost 200 calories per ounce.

A word about **whipping cream** Light whipping cream, often labeled simply "whipping cream," contains 30-36 percent butterfat; the less easily obtainable heavy whipping cream, or just "heavy cream," contains 36-40 percent fat. Both are fine for whipping and most cooking, but heavy cream is more suitable for desserts that are boiled or simmered—the more fat cream contains, the less likely it is to curdle.

Sweetened whipped cream There are several brands of ready-whipped cream on the market. It is mostly sold in aerosol cans, and contains a great deal of air and sugar. It tastes like soap.

Flour

This is not a baking book, so there is very little flour used in the recipes. I use white in preference to wholewheat. Use wholewheat instead if you wish, but don't blame me if your pastry tastes like an old cardboard box.

Eggs

All the recipes have been tested using extra large eggs. I can't think of any recipes in the book so delicately tuned that they will end in tears if your eggs are a size smaller or larger. This is not *haute cuisine*.

I remain a devotee of the free-range egg. I will use nothing else. I have seen for myself how hens are kept in cages, and found the whole egg production process positively distressing. I urge anyone with even the remotest conscience to buy free-range eggs. They taste better, anyway.

Chocolate

I also have strong feelings about chocolate, and particularly about the differences between "candy"-style chocolate and the real stuff. I go into it in more detail in the chocolate section.

THE PANTRY

A bare cupboard is not much use when you fancy something sweet. Even an egg or two and a jar of decent preserves will do—then at least you can have a fluffy, fruity sweet omelet. I list below a few oddments that I have found rather useful on days when I have failed yet again to come home with a handful of perfectly ripe figs or a slice of almond cake from the posh *pâtisserie*. Or perhaps I have, but still need a little something to make them special.

Lemons
For stopping cut fruit discoloring and for perking up almost anything. Particularly tropical fruits. An ex-editor friend of mine once told me, "even a tart has half a lemon in her refrigerator." I am not quite sure what she meant by "even." When you need to use lemon zest, try to buy organic or unwaxed lemons that have not been covered in pesticide.

Candied Citrus Peel
Huge crescent moons of orange, lemon, and citron peel for serving with coffee, or slicing and dipping into melted dark chocolate. Available from specialty stores.

Dried Figs, Raisins, and Prunes
Instant desserts, these look spectacular when piled high on platters.

Canned Figs
Green, in syrup.

Pistachios
Tantalizingly salty, dusty nuts blushed with purple, beige, and green. Bought in large bags in their shells, you may find they vaguely resemble the savory, addictive nuts you had on vacation. Bought ready-shelled, you might as well eat peanuts. The best seem to come from Lebanese markets, in large, unlabeled plastic bags. Generally speaking, the plumper the nut, the better the flavor. Shelling the little nuts after a soak in the bath will make your fingernails fray.

Almonds

Difficult nuts these. The best-tasting almonds are usually ones that you have shelled yourself, though how you break into the things is quite beyond me. If serving nuts for dessert it will be the almonds that are left when you clear away. Few can crack them. For cooking, ready-shelled ones should really be bought unskinned, and from a store with a high turnover. But skinning almonds is a drag at the best of times, and totally unsuitable in a book of fast food. Ground almonds are often best bought whole and unskinned, then ground in a blender, skin and all. That way they will be moist, unlike the majority of ground almonds in packages at the grocers.

Crystallized Violets and Rose Petals

The real thing, with a petal inside, and not the imitation ones made of confectioners' sugar and coloring. Try smart candy stores or bakeries.

Rosewater and Orange-Flower Water

Made from the distillation of rose petals and orange blossom. The soft, romantic fragrances add a magical perfume to fruits, creams, and syrups. Middle-Eastern brands are best, though Crabtree and Evelyn do a very fine rosewater, and by mail-order too. Stock up when you are next in a Turkish or Middle-Eastern market—most major cities have at least one. Again, you tend to get what you pay for, so go for broke.

Turkish Delight

The best I have ever eaten came from Istanbul via a friend who had been on a shopping trip. Chewy in the extreme and full of pistachios or scented with orange-flower or rosewater, I am virtually addicted to the stuff, late at night with little cups of strong coffee.

Marrons Glacés

For solitary moments of wanton extravagance.

M and M's

For sandwiches, made with white bread and a thin spreading of butter. Some people (they are usually rather Grand) claim not to like a handful of M and M's. I think they are lying.

Marshmallows
For toasting.

Honey
Again, you tend to get what you pay for. Cheap honey tastes of nothing but sugar—no flowery or herby notes, just sugar. Choose an herby honey, such as thyme or lavender, for recipes involving figs and prunes, and a flower one—orange blossom is the most accessible—for everything else. Liquid honeys are generally easier to work with, though set ones are best for spreading on fingers of bread and butter. Farmers' markets are a good source.

Preserves
Even the best preserves are not expensive. French-made preserves, thick with fruit and very little sugar, are good enough to eat straight from the spoon. Greengage, apricot, damson, and fig are my all-time favorites. French red-currant jellies are useful too, but make sure that the red-currant is crystal clear, slightly soft rather than set, and French. Many domestic versions taste of nothing but sugar and are as stiff as boards. Turkish rose-petal jam is good for spooning onto water biscuits with thick yogurt, and for dunking almond cookies into. It can be bought from Middle-Eastern markets and chic food emporiums. Cherry preserves, providing it is made from the tart little Morellos and not those candy-flavored sweet cherries, is just the thing for eating with *fromage blanc*—in alternate spoonfuls, straight from the jar.

Condensed Milk
Boiled in its can till thick. For serious sugar attacks.

Vanilla Beans
Actually the fruit of an orchid, sticky, dark vanilla beans give a softer, purer fragrance than even the best extracts. But they take a while to give up their flavor to creams and custards, so it is best to keep them in a jar of granulated sugar; the beans will scent the sugar, which can be used in or on almost anything. You can keep good beans for ages in a jar, continually replenishing the sugar as you use it. Once the beans have lost their clout, throw them out.

Vanilla Extract
If you have a bottle of something labeled vanilla flavoring or vanillin, throw it out, then go and buy a bottle of pure vanilla extract. Lacking the nasty chemical taste of the "flavoring," vanilla extract is basically made from vanilla beans soaked in an alcohol/water solution. American and French brands are very good. If you have never bought the real stuff before you may be shocked at what you will be asked to pay for it. It's worth it, and lasts for ages, tightly capped.

Unsweetened Cocoa Powder
Go for broke. Get the real thing. Sweetened cocoa powder will not do. For anything. Look for Dutch-process cocoa, which is richer and darker than other cocoa powders.

Spices
Fennel seeds, cinnamon (sticks and ground), nutmeg (whole), coriander seeds, and a few whole cloves.

Peppercorns
For bringing out the flavor of strawberries. Keep them whole till you need them to preserve their elusive aromatic warmth.

Balsamic Vinegar
For sprinkling in minute amounts over berries. Put it at the top of your Christmas list or treat yourself to a bottle, even if it is not the best. Who cares—its mellow richness will still do wonders for your berries.

Bath Olivers and Carr's Miniature Water Biscuits
Suitably bland vehicles for delicate preserves and soft cheeses. Ideal companions for quince jelly and thick cream or rose-petal jam and *fromage frais*. Try water biscuits heaped with spoonfuls of black-currant conserve and whipped cream, and Bath Olivers with figs and goat cheese.

Ladyfingers and *Amaretti*
Ladyfingers, biscotti, and crunchy sugar-coated *amaretti* are enormously useful to have. In dessert emergencies I have served the diminutive almondy cookies alongside coffee cups of melted

bittersweet chocolate for dipping. A memorable success made from an otherwise empty cupboard.

Some Shortcuts

Frozen Puff Pastry Wonderful. Even smart restaurants use it, though they probably won't admit it.

Frozen Piecrust Less successful; it is just not buttery enough.

Chocolate Cups I rarely use these—it's not really my style—but friends swear by these ready-made miniature chocolate cases. I might be tempted if the chocolate were better quality.

Chocolate Sauce There are one or two brands of very fine ready-made chocolate sauce. The sexiest sauce I have ever eaten comes in fat glass tubs from the better specialty food shops. I keep a pot of it in the refrigerator for accompanying ice creams and fruits such as poached pears. Fearfully expensive at first glance, it goes a long way and can be kept in the refrigerator for a little while and reheated in a few minutes. It is probably the finest convenience food I have come across.

Sponge Shortcakes Really quite horrible.

Ladyfingers A much better choice, even if they are usually as dry as a bone. Great for dipping into fools, and for trifle or *tiramisu*.

Canned Rice Pudding Cold, straight out of the can. Best eaten late at night when seriously drunk.

Wafers and Fancy Cookies Italian and German brands. Fine, if expensive, accompaniments for creams and fools, or for serving with coffee. Only masochists would make their own *cigarette russe*. Particularly good are those Italian wafer rolls filled with hazelnut and chocolate paste. Find them in specialty gourmet markets.

AUTUMN

My year is still punctuated by the old school semesters, though I cannot think why. Perhaps it's that I find the beginning of the calendar year, January and February, so difficult to get through that I wish the year to have a better start. Autumn is, without doubt, my favorite season; it's the smell in the air, and the comfort of lighting the first fire in the hearth.

This is the season of my favorite fruits: dusty, purple black damsons; golden greengages; plump, bloomy figs; and the second flush of blood red, velvety raspberries . . . not to mention the sweet Muscat grapes, tart little blackberries, and blush-skinned luscious pears that will end up on the table in some form or another. This is the time of year when everything seems to be so ripe as to be nearly alcoholic, that *framboise* scent that you get with raspberries or the musky sweetness of Muscat grapes.

This is also the season of The Crisp. You can keep your bread puddings and fruit shortcake, good rib-sticking things though they are. For me, the high point of the dessert-maker's year is when plums, blackberries, and apples are covered in a crisp, buttery topping and served hot from the dish. They can be on the table in half an hour if you make them in not too deep a dish.

This is also the time for pan-frying pippin apples in butter and sugar till caramelized, and serving them with cream. Autumn is for lazy hot desserts like roasted figs or broiled pears, a time for baking plums with sweet golden wine and dunking blackberries into glasses of deep red Italian Barolo. The time of year, too, for matching apples and pears to cheese for the most instant seasonal dessert of all.

BLACKBERRIES *see also page 179*

I hope you are looking at these recipes in late August because you have been out picking blackberries—or brambles—from the hedgerows and you have a nice basket of them. These are the best: their flavor intense and their juice copious. Then again you may have picked up a basket or two from the market on the way home, in which case they will almost certainly be larger, cultivated fruits pampered no doubt by the growers, but their flavor will be more elusive. They will still be good, though, and without the possibility that someone's labrador may have got to them first.

BLACKBERRIES MARINATED IN *CASSIS*

I have said before that I keep very few liqueurs in the house. *Crème de mûres,* which is the very essence of blackberries, is not one of them. But *crème de cassis*, the intensely fruity blackcurrant version, has a place on the shelf if only for stirring into glasses of white wine for Kir. A quick splash from the *cassis* bottle will transform a bowl of purple fruits into the most heady of delights.

Tip the blackberries, which should really be the fleshy cultivated variety this time, into a glass bowl. Pour over a couple of good glugs of *cassis* (or *crème de mûres* if you have it) and sprinkle with sugar. Leave to marinate for as long as you can. Serve with rich cream.

BLACKBERRIES WITH *FROMAGE BLANC* AND CREAM

If there are blackberries in season I often unmold a small amount of *fromage blanc* into the center of a plate, scatter a handful of blackberries around it, and then pour a stream of whipping cream over. The effect of the mildly piquant white cheese, the sweet cream, and the scent of the purple fruits is positively ambrosial.

BLACKBERRIES IN BAROLO

It doesn't have to be Barolo, but something rich and fruity is called for.

FOR 4

1 pound blackberries   *½ cinnamon stick*
  (3 heaped cups)   *a long wide strip of orange*
3 tablespoons sugar   *zest*
1¼ cups Barolo wine

Bring the fruit to a boil with the sugar, wine, and aromatics in a stainless-steel saucepan. Turn down the heat and simmer for 8 minutes. Serve warm or chilled.

BLACKBERRY-GIN SAUCE

A quick, alcoholic sauce made with juicy blackberries.

FOR 4

½ pound blackberries (1½ cups)   *1 tablespoon lemon juice*
6 tablespoons sugar   *1 tablespoon gin*

Put the fruit into a stainless-steel saucepan with the sugar, lemon juice, and gin. Bring to a boil, then simmer gently for a minute or two. Push through a strainer and serve hot over ice cream or with crêpes.

BLACKBERRIES AND CREAM

Cream, berries, and toasted nuts.

FOR 4

¾ cup blackberries   *⅓ cup shelled hazelnuts*
2 tablespoons liquid honey   *⅔ cup thick plain yogurt*
1 tablespoon Kirsch   *⅔ cup whipping cream*

Tip the blackberries into a bowl and pour the honey all over them. Gently stir in the Kirsch. Set aside for 15-20 minutes.

Toast the hazelnuts in a frying pan or under the broiler. When they are fragrant, rub off some of their papery skins and chop the nuts roughly.

Spoon the blackberries into individual glasses. Mix together the yogurt and cream. Spoon it over the fruit, cover the cream with chopped hazelnuts, and eat with a teaspoon. The cream may curdle slightly where it meets the fruit, but no matter.

BLACKBERRIES WITH ROSE CREAM AND ROSE PETALS

A romantic, fragrant plate.

Pile blackberries onto individual plates. Flavor whipping cream with a little rosewater, then spoon it around the berries. Scatter rose petals from the garden, deep red and fragrant (with their yellow heels snipped off), over the berries. Pass around some almond cookies such as *amaretti*.

BLACKBERRIES WITH BAY CREAM AND ALMONDS

If you are looking for a simple version of one of those piled-high-on-a-big-plate desserts that you get in smart restaurants, here it is. They would probably add a little almond cookie on the side (and no doubt the ubiquitous mint leaf), and so would I. Steeping bay leaves in cream was Sophie Grigson's idea. The rest is mine.

FOR 4

1 cup heavy cream
1 tablespoon sugar
2 bay leaves of a reasonable
   size

2 tablespoons sliced almonds
1 pound blackberries
   (3 heaped cups)
a little confectioners' sugar

Pour the cream into a small pan and add the sugar and the bay leaves. Bring to a boil, then turn the heat very low and simmer, almost imperceptibly, for 8 minutes.

Toast the sliced almonds until they are golden. Pile the berries in the center of four plates. Pour the bay cream through a strainer, then spoon around the berries. Scatter the almonds on top, and dust with a very little confectioners' sugar.

BLACKBERRIES AND APPLES *see also page 61*

Can there be a more comforting, feel-good combination of fruits? The very words blackberry and apple have a warm, loving, and homey ring about them. Early apples with some tartness to them and sweet little blackberries turn up in all sorts of English pies, tarts, and puddings, most of which would sit uncomfortably in this collection of fast desserts.

BLACKBERRY AND APPLE PURÉE

FOR 3-4

1 pound apples   *½ pound blackberries (1½ cups)*
1 teaspoon ground cinnamon

Core the apples and chop them coarsely. Throw them into a shallow pan, and add the spice and a couple of tablespoons of water. Cook over medium heat, stirring occasionally, till the fruit is soft. This will take about 20 minutes.

Whizz the mixture in a food processor or blender till smooth, but don't overprocess it. Stir in the blackberries, halved if they are particularly large. Stir with a fork so that their juice will stain the purée.

Serve warm, in glasses, with a spoonful of cream or thick plain yogurt on top (in which case it may make enough for 4).

Or, if you can, leave it to cool, then chill. Use as a sauce, perhaps thinned with a little apple juice, for a bakery-bought almond cake, or as a pudding.

PLUMS *see also page 60*

We had plum trees in the garden when I was growing up: gnarled, bent old trees covered with lichen, just like a story book orchard. There were deep scarlet, blue-skinned plums with squashy yellow flesh and taller, less rickety greengage trees, which my father called goldengages. When the sun shone you could see through the fruit as far as its pit inside the flesh. The fruit was sweet and juicy and used to smell slightly winy, and the trees were full of large, docile wasps. We made crisps, pies, and some glorious jam.

Now I buy my plums in a transparent plastic carton with a pretty sticker on it and a use-by date. Six perfect plums sitting on a little sheet of bubble-wrap, as if they were Fabergé eggs. At the height of the season, though, there are wooden crates of the things in my local street market. Red plums, purple plums, dusty damsons with yellow leaves, and, occasionally, green-gages. When I can shop during the day, I buy the loose fruit from the market, though more often than not I have to shop on the way home from work. Then it's the Fabergé eggs.

A PLATTER OF PLUMS

Plums come in all sizes and shades. A brilliant harlequin colored dessert can be made by piling an assortment of plums, scarlet and blue, orange and gold, purple and yellow green, on a large white platter. The plums should be ripe but far from squashy, perhaps just dribbling a hint of juice from their stems. Place them in the center of the table and let everyone help themselves. A glass of something golden and sweet would make the picture even prettier.

PLUMS WITH HONEY AND CRUMBS

Too many times have I brought plums home to find them less sweet than they looked. Here is the answer, based on an idea of Margaret Costa's. Wonderful, incidentally, with damsons, though the pits may annoy.

FOR 4

1½ pounds ripe plums	*4 tablespoons liquid honey*
1½ cups fresh white or	*4 tablespoons butter, melted*
brown bread crumbs,	*2 tablespoons brown sugar*
not too fine	

Cut the plums in half and pull out the pits, saving as many of the juices as you can by doing the whole thing over a dish. Mix just over half of the bread crumbs with the honey. Make alternate layers of plum halves and honeyed crumb in a baking dish, starting and ending with fruit.

Mix the remaining crumbs with the melted butter. Stir in the sugar and sprinkle the mixture over the fruit. Bake in a preheated 400°F oven till crisp and golden, about 25 minutes.

SAUTÉED PLUMS

You have a bag of ripe plums. You want a hot dessert. You have only 10 minutes.

Rinse the plums, then drop them into a shallow pan set over medium heat. Sprinkle lightly with sugar. Throw in a generous chunk of butter. Slam on the lid. Cook for 8 minutes, or until the plums start to split. Serve hot with whipping cream.

Plums Baked in Sauternes

Good with plums of any sort but even better with greengages, when you can find them. The point of this dessert is in the golden, fruity, winy juices that collect in the bottom of the dish and mingle with the cream.

FOR 3

2 tablespoons butter
6 tablespoons sugar
12 medium plums

a wineglass of Sauternes or
other sweet wine
light whipping cream, to serve

Rub the butter around the inside of a shallow baking dish, then sprinkle in the sugar. Add the plums and bake for 10 minutes in a preheated 400°F oven.

Tip the dish slightly and baste the plums with any juices in the bottom of the dish. Pour in the wine and return to the oven to bake till the plums are tender and the cooking juices bubbling, about 15-20 minutes depending on the ripeness of the plums.

Eat from deep bowls, with the buttery juices and a pitcher of cream.

Damson Plums

I have a soft spot for damsons, no doubt because of childhood memories of picking the little fruits on misty autumn mornings while waiting for the school bus. I cannot resist them when they appear in the markets in September and October, but I rarely have much time to do anything with them that involves pastry or jam-making, and so tend to use them in a compote or crisp.

Hard, dusty, purple-blue damsons can be turned into a richly colored, intensely flavored compote in 20 minutes or so. I know of no other fruit that can be transformed so magically by a few minutes' cooking.

Hot Damson Compote

Remove the little stems from the fruit, discarding any squashed ones. Put them in a saucepan, stainless steel for preference, and add a small amount of water to come no further than a third of the way up the sides of the pan, plus a generous quantity of sugar. Bring quickly to a boil, then turn down the heat and simmer gently till the fruits have burst their skins and the juices have worked with the sugar to produce a rich purple sauce, about 15 minutes. Serve hot with cream.

➤ Upend a measure of gin, or slightly less, into the compote as you bring it to the table. Stir gently

APPLES *see also page 26*

If you have an apple in the fruit bowl then you have a real fast dessert. It takes but a few minutes to slice and caramelize it with honey and butter, or pan-fry it with vine fruits and Calvados. If it is a truly fine fruit, crisp and aromatic, then it is good enough to eat as it is. Treat it with respect.

The apple is Britain's national fruit. It suits our climate and our taste, and I do think colder climates produce a better tasting apple. Finding a good apple is easier than it used to be. Many of the large supermarket chains have taken the lead to encourage growers to plant old-fashioned varieties whose strength is flavor rather than high yield. The response has been encouraging, though many greengrocers have yet to catch on, offering us only a choice of green or red. And both tasteless.

There are warning signs to a tasteless apple. It is usually sold unlabeled. The skin is invariably waxed and shiny. The worst, which is usually deep red, will be oversized and neatly stacked, perhaps even hand polished by a bored assistant. Bite through the tough, greasy skin, and you will find soft, watery flesh, with no detectable apple flavor. The saddest part of all is that these apples are what many of us have been brought up on, and accept uncomplainingly. I should love to force-feed my local supermarket buyer his red, insipid apples.

A fine apple, and by fine I mean deeply flavored, is not difficult to spot. It will probably have a visibly rough skin. It will not shine. Pick it up and sniff it; a tasty apple will generally have a definite scent to it. And it will probably be sold from a wooden crate. If you are lucky, your careful choice will be rewarded with old-fashioned apple flavors of strawberry, wine, aniseed, or nuts.

Eating Apples

Munch them in the hand by all means, but a really fine apple deserves a plate and a little knife, if not a linen napkin. You may find an apple's flavor is more pronounced when eaten at room temperature; there is no real reason to refrigerate them anyway. The fruit should be thoroughly wiped to remove the worst of the wretched pesticides and fungicides used nowadays.

The following recipes will work well with Rome, Winesap, Pippins or McIntosh apples, but you can use virtually any variety. Use red and golden delicious only if there is nothing else. Farmers markets are often a source of interesting, old-fashioned apple varieties.

Pan-Fried Apples

Sweet apples, fried in butter till golden, take barely 10 minutes and can be used in all manner of desserts.

FOR 2
4 tablespoons butter
1 pound apples, cored and
* chopped in 1-inch pieces*

Melt the butter in a shallow pan. Add the apple cubes and cook over medium to high heat till golden and tender, about 10 minutes. Turn the heat up near the end of cooking to crisp the outsides a little. Remove with a slotted spoon.

➤ Serve the apples hot, surrounded by a pool of cold, fresh cream

➤ Remove the apples from the pan; add ⅓-½ cup of fresh white or brown bread crumbs and fry in the apple butter till golden. Scatter over the apples and eat while hot

➤ Stuff the hot apples into a crêpe (page 40) and roll it up

➤ Add a tablespoon of liquid honey toward the end of cooking, then eat the sweet result with a side dish of cold thick yogurt

➤ Make an omelet as on page 99, using the apples as an alternative filling

CROISSANTS WITH HOT APPLES AND *CRÈME FRAÎCHE*

Minute for minute, probably the most delicious fast dessert in the book.

FOR 2

2 tablespoons butter	*2 large, flaky croissants*
1 large apple	*3 tablespoons* crème fraîche
2 tablespoons sugar	

Melt the butter in a shallow pan. Halve and core the apple and cut into about ten wedges. Cook the apple in the butter till tender, turning once to cook the other side, then add the sugar and cook over high heat till the mixture caramelizes.

Warm the croissants. Split each one in half and fill with the *crème fraîche* and the hot apple slices. Spoon any remaining buttery sauce over, and replace the top halves. Eat while still hot.

➤ Good though the matching of crumbly, flaking croissant with hot sticky apples and cold, slightly sour cream is, you may want to gild the lily. Try a spoonful of preserves, something with a bit more bite to it, such as blueberry or gooseberry, tucked inside with the apple. The jam should be high-fruit, low-sugar, and compatible with apple, i.e. blackberry or quince rather than raspberry or strawberry

APPLES WITH CARAMEL SAUCE

If the apple you have in the fruit bowl is not tasting as good as it might, turn it into a hot dessert with the addition of just some sugar and butter. Brandy in some form or another will lift this little dish onto a higher plane.

FOR 1

1 large apple
3-4 tablespoons butter
2-3 tablespoons sugar

1 tablespoon brandy,
  preferably Calvados
2 tablespoons heavy cream

Cut the apple into four from stem to flower end and remove the core. Melt the butter in a shallow pan. When it starts to sizzle add the apple pieces and turn down the heat. Cook the apples slowly until tender, taking care that the butter does not burn. Remove the apples with a slotted spoon to a warm plate.

Sprinkle in the sugar, the amount depending on how sweet you want your sauce to be. Let the butter and sugar caramelize and start to turn golden. Add the brandy and cream. Allow the sauce to bubble for a minute, then spoon it over the apples. You may have a little too much sauce. You can always dunk your bread in it.

Apple Toasts with Apricot-Caramel Sauce

This slightly more substantial version of the previous recipe has a stickiness about it that demands sharp *crème fraîche* or thick plain yogurt on the side.

FOR EACH PERSON

1 large apple
3 tablespoons butter
2 tablespoons brown
  or granulated sugar
1 slice of bread cut from a
  crusty loaf

1 heaped tablespoon apricot
  preserves
a squeeze of lemon
1 heaped tablespoon crème
  fraîche *or thick yogurt*

Peel the apple, slice into eight pieces, and remove the core. Melt the butter in a shallow pan over medium heat. Add the sugar and when it dissolves tip in the apple pieces. Simmer for 8 minutes until tender and fluffy. Take care not to let the sugar and butter burn.

Meanwhile, toast the bread till golden. When the apple is ready, remove from the pan with a slotted spoon and put on the hot toast.

Place the apricot preserves in the pan, turn up the heat, and stir for 1 minute until it has melted into the caramel sauce. Add a squeeze or two of lemon juice; taste and add more if you like. Pour immediately over the apples and toast, and eat while hot with a dollop of yogurt or cream, thick and cold from the refrigerator.

Broiled Apples

A recipe based on one for pears in Patricia Hegarty's *An English Flavour*, an inspiring book by a cook who grows almost all her own fruit, vegetables, and herbs, including a selection of old-fashioned apples such as the local Worcester Pearmain.

FOR 2

2 apples   *2 tablespoons butter, melted*
juice of ½ lemon   *1 tablespoon liquid honey*

Peel the apples and halve them from stem to flower end. Cut out the core. Brush all over with lemon juice, then lay the fruit, cut-side down, on a broiler rack. Brush with the butter.

Broil, about 4 inches away from the heat, until the apples begin to brown, about 10 minutes. Turn them over, brush with butter, and broil until the apples start to color. Pour the honey into the hollows where the cores were, and return to the broiler. When the honey bubbles, and the apples are tender to the point of a knife, they are done. Eat with cream or ice cream.

Apple Purée

A bowl of apple puree is simple enough to make and is a good thing to have around, as a base for quick desserts of all sorts.

MAKES ABOUT 11/4-11/2 CUPS

1¼ pounds baking apples   *½ teaspoon pumpkin-pie spice*
1 teaspoon ground cinnamon

Cut the apples in half, remove the cores, and then chop roughly. The pieces can be quite large. Throw them into a shallow pan with the spices and a couple of tablespoons of water (or apple cider if there is some around).

Set the pan over low to medium heat and cook, stirring or shaking the pan occasionally, and checking that nothing has stuck. Add a little more liquid if it looks as though it needs it; the mixture is done when the apples are reduced to a thick mush, about 20 minutes, perhaps less.

Whizz in the food processor or blender for a few seconds till smooth. But stop before it turns to baby food.

A Few Things to do with Apple Purée

➤ Serve the purée as it is, on a soup plate, stirring in a dollop of thick plain yogurt or cream

➤ Spread onto hot buttered toast for a snack

➤ Chilled, as a dip for coarse, crisp oatcakes

➤ As a sauce for a plain almond sponge cake, which you will have bought from a very expensive bakery on the way home

Apple-Yogurt Fool

FOR 4

*the apple purée opposite,
    chilled, sweetened with
    1 tablespoon liquid honey*

*1 cup thick plain yogurt or use
    ½ cup yogurt and
    ½ cup softly whipped cream
    1 tablespoon liquid honey*

Stir the chilled and sweetened purée into the yogurt or yogurt and cream mixture. Spoon into four wineglasses and leave in the refrigerator as long as you can; half an hour would be ideal. Drizzle a little more honey on top, and eat with crisp almond cookies.

➤ If you want to put something else on top I suggest a sprinkling of sliced almonds toasted till golden brown, or a scattering of bread crumbs, cooked in butter till golden and crisp

Apple Snow with Maple-Syrup Sauce

FOR 4

*⅔ cup maple syrup
½ cup heavy cream
6 tablespoons butter*

*2 extra large egg whites
½ teaspoon cream of tartar
the apple purée opposite*

Place the maple syrup, cream, and butter in a small pan and simmer over medium heat till slightly thickened, stirring from time to time. This will take about 10 minutes. Pour into a cool bowl and set aside.

Beat the egg whites with the cream of tartar till they form stiff peaks. Gently and slowly beat in the apple purée, a little at a time. The mixture should be soft enough to hold its shape in a spoon.

Divide the mixture among four wineglasses. Chill till required. When you are ready to eat, stir the maple-syrup sauce, and spoon some of it over the apple snow. You may have too much. It will keep, refrigerated, for a couple of days.

GOLDEN, FRAGRANT BAKED APPLES

This version of baked apples is a finer thing altogether than the usual ones stuffed with mincemeat, which are too often watery and oversweet. Choose large apples—something aromatic such as pippins or winesap would be perfect—and you will have fluffy, golden globes within the half hour. One of my favorite recipes in the book.

FOR 2

2 large apples, pippins or winesap
2 walnut-sized pieces of
   butter
juice of 1 orange

1 juicy passion fruit
   (lightly wrinkled and
   heavy for its size)

Heat the oven to 425°F. Core the apples with an apple corer or small knife. Cut a line around the circumference of each apple, just deep enough to pierce the skin. Place in a small flat dish and put a piece of butter in each cavity. Squeeze the orange juice over and put in the hot oven.

Bake for 25 minutes till the skin is golden and the fruit is puffed up and fluffy. Remove from the oven and immediately squeeze half a passion fruit over each apple, seeds and all. Eat while the apples are still hot and deeply fragrant from the butter, orange, and passion fruit.

Quick Apple Tarts

These little tarts take a matter of minutes to make. They are at their best when cooked slightly more than you would think, so that the pastry is very crisp and the apples lightly caramelized. I usually eat these with thick cream.

FOR 2

*5 ounces puff pastry
(thawed if frozen)
2 medium apples, peeled
and cored*

*2 tablespoons butter, melted
1 tablespoon sugar
2 tablespoons apricot, greengage,
or fig preserves warmed*

Preheat the oven to 425°F. Put a baking sheet into the oven to heat. (The point of this is to ensure that the base of the tarts is cooked thoroughly.) Cut the pastry in half and roll out each square large enough to cut a disk of pastry about 6½ inches in diameter. That's about the size of a side plate.

Slice the apples thinly. Prick the pastry disks four or five times to stop them puffing up and tossing the apples onto the baking sheet. Place the apples, neatly if you have time, on the pastry, leaving a clear border about 1 inch wide. Brush the apples and the pastry with butter without letting the butter drizzle down the sides of the pastry, which may prevent it rising.

Sprinkle the sugar over and transfer the tarts to the hot baking sheet. The easiest way to do this is to remove the baking sheet from the oven and lift on each tart using a spatula, plus a bit of help from your fingers. Leave as much space on the sheet between the tarts as possible. Bake for 15 minutes. Remove the sheet from the oven and pour the warmed preserves over. Return to the oven for 4 or 5 minutes till the preserves are bubbling, the pastry is crisp, and the apples slightly browned at the edges.

Apple Crêpes

If you have eggs in the kitchen and apples in the fruit bowl then you have a real fast dessert.

FOR 4

¾ cup all-purpose flour
salt
1 tablespoon sugar
3 eggs
1 cup milk

4 small apples
1-2 tablespoons butter, melted
butter, for frying
sugar, for sprinkling

Whizz the flour, salt, sugar, eggs, and milk in the blender or food processor till smooth. A matter of seconds. Or, whisk them together by hand if you prefer. The resulting batter should be the same consistency as heavy cream. Add a little water if it is too thick. Set aside for as near to 30 minutes as you can, although 10 will do.

Remove the cores from the apples. An apple corer will help, though you can use a long-bladed small knife if you can't find the corer. (It will be at the very back of the drawer, with the rusty piping tubes.) Slice the apples in thin rounds.

Stir the melted butter into the batter. Melt a little butter in a suitable pan. I cook crêpes in my omelet pan, which is now so old and seasoned that I can even scrub it clean and it rarely sticks. Ideally, the pan should be about 8 inches in diameter and with slightly turned up edges. A frying pan will be fine as long as you know it doesn't stick.

When the butter sizzles, pour out any that is more than just a thin coating, then pour in enough batter to coat the bottom thinly. It does not matter if the crêpe has a few holes; in fact, I regard them as something of a plus. (There are very detailed crêpe-making directions on page 100.) As the batter starts to cook, add a few of the apple rings in a single layer. Pour over more batter to cover the apples and cook for a minute till lightly set.

Turn the crêpe over. This is easy enough to do with a large, flat spatula or pancake turner, though I always use my fingers as well. Flipping it over quickly has always proved more successful for me than dithering about, expecting it to break. Cook the remaining side and serve warm, sprinkled with a little sugar. Repeat with the other apples and the remaining batter.

Praline Ice Cream with Hot Apples, Honey, and Spices

I love desserts that marry the blisteringly hot with the icy cold. Vanilla ice cream with hot chocolate sauce is one; this fruity sauce, which smells like baked apples, is another. A nutty ice cream, such as walnut or almond-rich praline, would not be too much here, though vanilla would be fine. The ice cream should be very cold.

FOR 2, GENEROUSLY

1 pound apples
3-4 tablespoons butter
3 tablespoons liquid honey
pinch of ground cinnamon

pinch of pumpkin-pie spice
½ cup large, juicy raisins
vanilla or praline ice cream
*   for 2*

Cut the apples—it will probably be about two large ones—into four. Take out the cores and cut each piece of apple in chunks. Melt the butter with the honey in a shallow pan. Add the spices. Leave the sauce to bubble over medium heat for a minute or so, stirring occasionally. Add the apples and raisins.

Turn the heat so that the apples are just simmering. Cook for 7-10 minutes till they are tender. Place a large ball of ice cream on each plate, then spoon around the hot fruit. Pour the bubbling sauce over the ice cream and eat immediately to make the most of the startling contrast in texture.

Pan-Fried Apple and Cheshire Cheese Savory

FOR 2

1 large or 2 small apples
juice of ½ lemon
1 tablespoon walnut oil
2 tablespoons shelled walnuts

a handful of salad leaves such
 as Belgian endive
3-4 ounces Cheshire cheese

Wipe the apples but don't bother peeling them. Cut them in half and then in quarters. Remove the cores and cut each apple in thick slices, probably about eight per apple. Squeeze a little lemon juice onto the flesh to stop it discoloring.

Warm the oil in a shallow pan, place the apple slices in the pan, and scatter the walnuts over. Cook over medium heat until the apples are golden and tender and the walnuts are fragrant, about 5 minutes, turning them once. Place a few salad leaves on each of two plates. Remove the apples with a metal spatula and place on top of the leaves.

Crumble the cheese into small lumps, about the size of walnut halves, and scatter immediately over the hot apples. The cheese will soften slightly. Pour any remaining lemon juice into the pan, turn up the heat, and scrape any bits stuck on the pan into the dressing. Bubble for a couple of seconds, then pour the pan juices (there won't be a lot) and walnuts over the cheese and apples.

Apples and Cheese

I am convinced that apples and cheese were created for each other—a marriage made in heaven as far as I am concerned.

PEARS

To finish an autumn supper with a single aromatic pear, golden-skinned and freckly, with buttery, juicy flesh, can be a great joy. If the fruit is really fine, it can be eaten for lunch with nothing more than a piece of cheese and some crusty, open-textured bread.

It can be difficult to catch pears at their point of perfection, when they are at their most juicy and sweet. You have to keep an eye on them. Like so many fruits, I find it best to buy them slightly underripe and finish them off at home. Although I like the bland crunch of a hard, glassy pear, that is hardly when they are at their best. Most yield more flavor when they are blushed and turning slightly yellow, though it is as well to remember that at this point they bruise as easily as a peach.

In the autumn most markets will offer a couple of varieties of pear; if you are lucky it will be Williams' Bon Chrétien (called Bartletts in the U.S.) and Doyenne du Comice.

Comice pears are plump and blunt, greenish-yellow in color with a red blush. They are one of the sweetest pears and highly fragrant, a perfect dessert fruit. Bartlett is another fat, rounded pear that turns yellow-blush as it ripens. Conference, a tapered green and russet pear, is found in late autumn and early winter in the U.K. It has a nutty flavor and a grainy texture that I like very much with cheese.

A PLATE OF PEARS

Choose ripe, juicy pears, Bartlett or Comice perhaps. They should be firm enough to be picked up easily when sliced but ripe enough to dribble a little when you peel them. Except you are not going to peel them. Cut the pears in half lengthwise and in half again, then remove the cores. Place the pear pieces on a white plate: they can be arranged prettily or piled any old way, but they should have their fleshy side up, skin side down.

Get out the *eau de vie* bottle. *Poire Williams* would be wonderful, but *framboise*, which is the very essence of crushed raspberries, is surprisingly good here too. Covering most of the open bottle neck with your thumb, sprinkle a little of the heavenly scented liquor over the fruit. Serve slightly chilled.

You may want to rub the cut side of the fruit with half a lemon if you are going to leave the fruit to chill for any length of time.

➤ I tried this with Calvados, the apple brandy, but the alcohol hid rather than flattered the fruit

➤ If ever you come across a pear sorbet at one of those posh gourmet stores, then bring it home and eat it in chilled bowls surrounded by slices of pears and *Poire Williams eau de vie*

Pears with Almonds or Hazelnuts

A lovely idea from Lynda Brown, which takes the pears and *Poire Williams* idea slightly further. To the above recipe, if you can call it that, add a handful of toasted almonds or hazelnuts, rubbed in a dish towel to remove their skins, and chopped coarsely.

Pears and Pepper

Try grinding a little black pepper over quarters of ripe pear. Not too much, and not too fine, just enough to bring out the flavor.

Pears and Peppercorns

Soft green peppercorns, aromatic and a little hot, are sold in specialty grocers in jars of brine. I have taken to crushing a few drained ones with the back of a spoon (say half-a-dozen for each pear) and spreading them somewhat haphazardly over halves of the fruit. More of a snack than a dessert.

A Little Trick with Pears

If you have bought pears that are far from ripe you can bring them to perfection more quickly if you keep them in a paper bag with—and this is not a myth—a ripe apple. Do not seal the bag fully (leave a little hole in the top) and put it in a warm, but far from hot, place. The pears will ripen much faster than if left to their own devices.

A Pear Snack

Something to nibble on your own. Wipe and quarter a ripe pear, remove the core, and then dip the fruit, each piece as you eat it, into liquid, golden honey. Chestnut is my favorite for this, but orange-blossom or heather honey can be good too. Give the medicinal eucalyptus honey a miss.

Baked Pears with Vanilla Ice Cream

Although this buttery, fruity dessert stretches the thirty minute limit to the full, I include it because of its ease of preparation and the delicious way the hot, sweet pear juices mingle with the cold ice cream. Use the very best vanilla ice cream you can buy.

FOR 4

4 large, juicy pears	*4 tablespoons butter, melted*
¼ cup sugar	*good quality vanilla ice*
1 tablespoon lemon juice	*cream, straight from*
a vanilla bean	*the freezer*

Peel and core the pears and cut them in thin slices. Toss them into an ovenproof dish with the sugar, lemon juice, vanilla bean, and melted butter. Level the pears and bake in a preheated 400°F oven for about 30 minutes, until tender and golden. A couple of times during cooking, tip the dish slightly and baste the pears with the cooking juices.

Place a scoop of ice cream on each of four plates, surround with the hot fruit, and spoon the rich, buttery juices over the soft, hot pears and the cold, hard ice cream.

A Cream to Serve with Ripe Pears

An idea from a favorite cookbook, *Chez Panisse Cooking* by Alice Waters.

I cannot explain why black currants, normally so bullying and intensely flavored, flatter pears in the way they do. Here, a liqueur made from the fruit (and one of the few I have in the cupboard), is folded into a cream to accompany slices of juicy, honey-fleshed pear.

Whip 1 cup of cream till it stands in soft peaks, just short of what you would normally call softly whipped. Fold in a couple of tablespoons of *crème de cassis*, the stuff you use in Kir, a little at a time, and mix slowly until it has scented the cream.

PEARS WITH SOFT CHEESES

Creamy, sweet soft cheeses partner pears perfectly. Mascarpone, the rich and thick Italian cream cheese, or even the white and lumpy cottage cheese from the supermarket can turn a pear into a dessert in minutes. There is something that works for me about the graininess of the pear, and the smoothness of the cheese.

PEARS WITH MASCARPONE

Choose ripe, juicy pears and mascarpone cheese at room temperature. Comice would be perfect for this. Allow one fruit per person, wipe it, and cut it in quarters from core to flower end. Remove the core, then place on a large plate. Put a dish of mascarpone cheese in the center and let everyone dip their pears in the cheese.

WARM PEARS WITH MELTED MASCARPONE

FOR 2

2 ripe Comice pears *4 ounces mascarpone cheese (about ½ cup)*

Quarter the pears and core them. Place the fruit, skin-side down, in a shallow heatproof dish. Spoon a dollop of mascarpone cheese over each quarter, then place under a preheated broiler, about 5 inches from the heat, till it melts. Serve while the cheese is still soft and runny.

PEARS WITH BLUE CHEESE

Blue-veined cheeses can be just as good with pears as hard Parmesan and soft cream cheeses. One of my favorite desserts is a ripe, honey-sweet pear with a slice of gorgonzola or a lump of Stilton. When I can afford Roquefort, the French blue cheese with a salty bite, I often buy pears to enjoy with it at the same time.

Pears with Walnuts and Blue Cheese

I leave the choice of cheese to you. Cashel Blue, the soft and creamy Irish cheese, or tangy Maytag Blue from the United States will marry as happily with pears as a lump of deeply flavored gorgonzola. The fastest way to serve them is to place a large piece of the blue-veined cheese in the center of the table with a plate of yellow and blush-pink pears. Scatter a few whole walnuts around and let everyone sort it out for themselves.

With a little more time you could make individual plates of sliced cheese and wiped, quartered, and cored fruit. And you could remove the walnuts from their shells.

Lockets' Savoury

Lockets was one of those masculine London restaurants that served "comfort" food to Members of Parliament. This was the place to come for asparagus, salmon, and strawberries in season. The dessert cart was, by all accounts, not worth bothering with (when are they?), so diners tended to finish their meals with cheese or something hot from the kitchen. They would then, no doubt, doze off until woken by the House of Commons division bell. Even the 1971 *Good Food Guide* noted it was: "within shuffling distance of the House of Commons." Lockets' Savoury must have been what they did with the ends of the Stilton.

FOR 2, AS A SAVORY OR SNACK

2 thickish slices of white bread cut from a decent crusty loaf	*1 large ripe pear, peeled and cored*
a few sprigs of watercress	*freshly ground black pepper*
	5 ounces Stilton cheese

Toast the bread, then remove the crusts if you want to give the dish a modicum of elegance. Divide the watercress between the two slices of toast. Slice the pear thinly and arrange the fruit on the toast. Season with a little freshly ground pepper. Remove thick shavings of Stilton with a potato peeler and arrange them over the pear, then place in a preheated 400°F oven till the cheese is melting. Eat warm.

Pears with Hard Cheeses

Pears with Pecorino

Pecorino is an Italian cheese made from sheep's milk, though it is not dissimilar in flavor to a young Parmesan. In Tuscany, it is traditionally eaten with pears, at the end of a meal.

Young ricotta pecorino is the one you want to eat as dessert—tell your cheesemonger, otherwise he'll sell you the harder, though even tastier, pecorino romano. Ask to taste it: it should be not too salty and soft enough to slice with a potato peeler. Buy a fair-sized lump that will last for a couple of meals. Should you fail to use it all quickly enough, it makes a grating cheese almost as good as Parmesan.

Choose pears that are really ripe; hard fruit will ruin this dish. Go by smell, which should be sweet. Use one fruit per person. Wipe the pears but do not peel them. Slice them in quarters from stem to flower end. Slice out the core and set them on a plate, sprinkling with a little lemon juice to keep them from browning.

Using a vegetable peeler, take thick shavings, as large as you can, from the cut side of the cheese and lay these on the plate with the pears. Eat while the pears are still moist.

Let's Take the Idea a Little Further . . .

Pears with Melted Pecorino

As before, the fruit must be really ripe. Use young Parmesan if you prefer.

Halve the pears, core, and peel them. Lay each half flat on the bottom of the broiler pan. Holding the pear in shape with one hand, cut the pear in thin slices. Cut a slice of pecorino with a vegetable peeler or sharp knife for each pear half. Lay the cheese over the fruit.

Place under a preheated broiler until the cheese starts to melt a little (it won't bubble like Cheddar would). When it browns very slightly in patches, remove from the heat and lift onto plates using a large, flat spatula or pancake turner. Eat hot.

Hard Pears and Aged Parmesan

There is a difference between a firm and a hard pear. Firm pears yield slightly when squeezed and soften after 20 minutes' cooking. Hard pears are made edible only by long poaching in a sweet syrup, possibly containing wine and aromatics. When you bravely bite into them raw their flesh will be hard, white, and glassy; there may be flavor, but there will be no perfume. Tapered Conference pears are more likely to be hard. They have no real place in this book other than for me to mention that I occasionally buy them just to match their grainy, crisp flesh with a piece of equally grainy and crisp, aged Parmesan—the sort you would usually grate. A deeply savory combination that makes the veins stand out on the roof of your mouth.

Marrons Glacés

A plate of frosted, mealy *marron glacés* is a treat indeed. The whole chestnuts are soaked in syrup and dried over and over again until they develop a melting consistency within and a crisp, sugary outer shell. Forget what anyone tells you about them being expensive and disappointing. They are talking nonsense. *Marrons glacés* are a delicacy, in the true sense of the word. And, like all true delicacies, they are fearfully, outrageously expensive.

Should you have a surplus of the things (I cannot imagine why) or should you need to make a few stretch a long way, then there are one or two possibilities. I must admit, though, that if I had only a few *marrons glacés* to serve my guests I would give them something else, and wolf the *marrons* myself. In secret.

➤ Crush the *marrons* with a fork, using, say, one per person. Mix with a heaped tablespoon of softly whipped cream per person and a splash, no more, from the brandy bottle. Spread on tiny, store-bought macaroons or sugared ladyfingers, but not *amaretti*, which are too strongly flavored, and eat with coffee. Don't try this for less than four. You cannot whip a smaller quantity of cream successfully. At least, I can't

➤ Crumble, rather than crush, the *marrons*. Stir them into cream that has been whipped into thick waves. Set aside for 20 minutes, then spoon in dollops with French fig preserves, onto thin slices of crackly baguette

... AND A LITTLE FURTHER STILL ...

PEARS WITH MELTED PECORINO AND CHESTNUT HONEY

When I first saw this on an Italian restaurant menu I was extremely suspicious, and ordered it out of curiosity.

It is surprisingly delicious, and is, in essence, no different from traditional marriages of savory and sweet like Cheshire cheese with sweet fruit cake or the Spanish snack of Manchego cheese with quince paste.

FOR EACH PERSON

½ large, very ripe pear
2 large slices of pecorino or
  Parmesan cheese

1 tablespoon liquid honey,
  preferably chestnut
a little confectioners' sugar

Heat the broiler. Peel the pear. Halve and core it. Place each half flat down on the broiler pan and slice it thinly as in the preceding recipe. Place the cheese slices on the pear, drizzle the honey over, and broil till bubbling. Dust very lightly with confectioners' sugar. Eat while still warm.

PEARS WITH PARMESAN AND WALNUTS

I prefer a slightly firmer pear with this savory, bordering on the pungent, cheese. Young Parmesan cheese can be peeled in large wafers with a vegetable peeler. Always buy imported Italian Parmigiano-Reggiano, choosing a less-aged one for this dish.

Wipe the pears, which might be ripe and granular-fleshed ones, quarter them, and remove the cores. I particularly enjoy the slightly rough, dry skin of Conference pears, though some may prefer to remove it. Lay the pears on a plate, cut in thinner pieces if you like, and cover with thin wafers, or shavings if your skill with the peeler wasn't up to much, of Parmesan. Scatter freshly shelled walnut halves over the cheese.

➤ If I am eating alone I will just break off a piece of Parmesan and munch it with the pear. In this case I will probably be eating it for lunch rather than as an after-dinner savory

CHESTNUT PURÉE

People seem divided over chestnut purée, in much the same way as they are over chicken livers or gooseberries. I have known some to go into complete ecstasy over a bowlful, lightly sweetened with confectioners' sugar and topped with whipped cream, sundae-style. Others have likened the stuff to dog food.

Chestnut purée is best made with fresh chestnuts, which you will have peeled yourself. You will probably have shriveled your fingers in the hot soaking water and torn your nails to shreds, too. Your hands will look like something from an Edgar Allan Poe story. Just this once, forget the best for the sake of speed and go for second best: the canned, unsweetened stuff.

Don't be put off by the dull browny-gray lump. It is just a starting point and needs a little embellishment. Brandy, say, or sherry, plus a bit of sugar, thick fluffy cream, and, perhaps, melted chocolate. I have known those who can enjoy it straight from the can.

CHESTNUT CREAM

Mix a can of chestnut purée with an equal quantity of whipped cream. Easy enough to do if you tip the contents of the can into a bowl, mash it into submission with a large fork, and half fill the empty can with whipping cream. Whip the cream slowly till thick and almost at the point where it stands in peaks. Fold carefully into the nut purée.

Add a drop or two (I should make it two, at least) of brandy, and stir in. Taste it, and add some confectioners' sugar, if you think it needs it. It probably will. Spoon into glasses and serve with a thin, posh cookie. One of those cigarette wafers filled with chocolate truffle would be nice.

➤ Top each glass with shavings of dark chocolate

➤ Best served in small amounts, because it really is rather rich

CHOCOLATE-CHESTNUT CREAM

A rather luxurious dessert for a cool, late autumn night.

FOR 4

6 ounces semisweet chocolate
1½ cups chestnut purée
1 tablespoon confectioners'
  sugar

1 cup whipping cream
unsweetened cocoa powder,
  to sprinkle

Break the chocolate into pieces and melt in a small bowl over hot water. There are full instructions for melting chocolate in the chocolate section on page 128. Crush the chestnut purée with a fork and stir in the confectioners' sugar. Gently stir in the melted chocolate.

Put the chocolate-chestnut mixture in the refrigerator while you whip the cream into soft drifts rather than stiff peaks. Leave the chocolate-chestnut mixture for 10 minutes, or more if you have time, then spoon into glasses. Top with spoonfuls of whipped cream and sprinkle with cocoa powder. Make sure it's the proper stuff.

➤ Gild the lily even further by scattering toasted sliced almonds on top of the cream

➤ After a rich main dish this will stretch to 6, if served in small glasses

GRAPES

If anyone tells you that grapes are good when cooked I suggest you treat them with suspicion. Grapes, at least in my house, are to be eaten from the vine, at the table, if not from the bag on the way home. My favorite way to present them is in a bowlful of ice water. Then the fruit gets really cold and the skins get tight and each grape seems to burst when you bite into it, exploding with its sweet juice.

It is the late-season muscat grapes that particularly excite me. Catching them at their peak is easy enough; just let them go very yellow before eating them. That way they will be at their sweetest.

Italia grapes, but eat them only when they are truly golden—
there is little pleasure to be had in underripe grapes. Red grapes
are rarely as good as they look.

From time to time I buy a bunch of big black ones, but they
have no real flavor. The silly little green seedless ones can be fun,
though hardly a gastronomic treat. Grapes have a better flavor
the nearer they are to rotting.

FIGS *see also page 103*

Figs are perfect for the fast foodie. They respond well to a small
amount of heat, their flavor reaching its height when they are
warm. Long cooking does them no favors at all.

They are for me one of the finest flavored fruits, scarlet
fleshed, sensual things that they are. I rank them up there with
ripe, cold muscat grapes, raspberries and mulberries, dribbling
peaches, and perfumed Charentais melons. It is hard to find a
fruit that is such a joy to look at, let alone eat.

I have to say I prefer the purple to the green, and the fatter
and squatter the better. If they look swollen, sore even, they are
probably going to be good to eat; if they look as though they are
about to burst and have glistening beads of stickiness from the
flower end, then they could be sublime.

Even the names of the varieties are a joy to read: Negronne,
Negro Largo, and Violette de Bordeaux. There is one named
Madonna. There is no doubting its sexiness, though I have read
enough purple prose about fig-eating to excite me for a lifetime.

FIGS ON *CIABATTA*

Ciabatta, the open-textured, slipper-shaped Italian bread, pro-
vides a chewy base for a snack of figs. Simply break off pieces of
the bread and munch them with the ripe figs.

A FEW FACTS ABOUT FIGS

➤ There are few figs that need peeling; the skin is almost always
edible

➤ The heavier the fig, the more succulent it is likely to be

➤ Figs taste better when they are warm; leave them in the sun before eating if you can

➤ Figs are totally wasted in a fruit salad

➤ If you are looking for a cheese to match with figs, then you will do no better than a Brie, preferably on the firm side

➤ Figs have an affinity with yogurt, clotted cream, cream cheeses, honey, raspberries (and I would add blackberries), and herbs such as thyme and lavender. Oh, and walnuts

➤ If I am feeling even lazier than usual, I will sometimes tear a fig in half, spread on a small amount of cream or cottage cheese, and eat it as I clear away the supper things

FIGS WITH RASPBERRIES AND CREAM

Big purple figs, as fat as they come, and deep-red raspberries marry beautifully with golden, crusty clotted cream, or with the richest whipped cream.

Place the figs on a large plate, allowing two large fruits per person. Make a slit in the top of each fig and press the sides gently. It will open up like a water lily. Place a scoop of clotted cream into each fig. Scatter the ripe raspberries over—they must be really ripe—and serve.

FIGS WITH *FRAISES DES BOIS*

My local superdooper-supermarket carries *fraises des bois* early in the autumn. But don't expect to buy them everywhere. They twinkle like stars when scattered over a plate of open figs. Slit the figs and press them to open, then drop the little wild strawberries over the singing figs, as if you are feeding baby birds in the nest. If you judged the ripeness correctly, they will need no yogurt, cream, or honey. Just a glass of something golden and sticky.

ROASTED FIGS

FOR 2

6 plump, purple figs   4 heaped tablespoons sugar
butter

Place the figs snugly in a generously buttered shallow dish.
Sprinkle with a tablespoon of water and half of the sugar and bake
in a preheated 400°F oven for 15 minutes. Baste the figs with the
syrup in the dish, then sprinkle the remaining sugar over. Bake for
a further 5 minutes. Serve hot or warm, with cream or yogurt.

FIGS BAKED WITH HONEY AND LEMON

FOR 2

6 fat, purple figs   juice of ½ lemon
3 tablespoons liquid honey

Put the figs in a shallow baking dish; they should nestle up
against each other. Pour the honey and the lemon juice over.
Bake for 20 minutes in a preheated 400° oven, occasionally bast-
ing the fruit with the juices in the dish. Serve warm, perhaps
with thick plain yogurt.

BAKED FIGS WITH MASCARPONE AND WALNUTS

FOR 4

12 ripe figs   2 tablespoons Marsala or
½ cup broken walnut pieces   medium sherry
3 tablespoons liquid honey—   ½ cup mascarpone cheese
    an herbal one would be nice

Cut a deep cross in the top of each fig and gently push the sides
to open a hollow in each fig.
    Toast the walnuts lightly under the broiler till fragrant but
barely colored. Rub off any of the skins that have come loose
(there is no need to be too pernickety about this). Mix the
broken nuts with the honey, alcohol, and mascarpone cheese.
Fill the figs with the nut mixture.

Bake in a preheated 400°F oven until bubbling, about 15 minutes. Serve warm.

More Figs with Mascarpone and Walnuts

Cut ripe figs in half, two or three halves per person depending on their size, and lay them on a large plate. Mix 3 heaped table-spoons of mascarpone cheese per person with enough cream to make it spoonable but still voluptuous. Place a spoonful of the softened mascarpone on each fig half, then scatter chopped toasted walnuts over. Drizzle with a little herb honey—thyme or lavender would be more than suitable—and serve outdoors, in the autumn sunshine.

A Plate of Purple Autumn Fruits

A neighbor of mine has a fig tree. The fruit never seems to come to anything, and in September the tree drops its tiny unripe fruit all over the sidewalk. I have forgotten how many times I have slipped on the things coming home with bags of shopping. But the leaves are a great asset. Apart from using them as cheese plates for little ash-covered goat cheeses and other photographic presentations I have used them to great effect under fruit.

Pears look wonderful on a plate of fig leaves and so, not surprisingly, do figs. A favorite plate of mine to offer after dinner is one that includes dark purple figs scattered with the last of the blackberries and a handful of pastel-colored sugared almonds. This particular plate is to be eaten before, rather than with, coffee.

Dried Figs

My favorite of all the dried fruits. The best, by which I mean the softest textured and the most intensely flavored, come from Turkey. Expect the autumn harvest to be in the markets at the end of November and to remain in good condition until early spring. The ones sold loose from cartons in specialist and ethnic food stores are invariably better than the squashed lumps in plastic bags from the healthfood store. Only the former are suitable to eat as dessert or as a sweet snack.

FIGS AND FENNEL SEEDS

Allow about four plump dried figs per person. Eat one first, and if it has a hard stem tucked inside it then you will have to remove them all, one by one. But this is not difficult or particularly time-consuming. Scissors or a small sharp knife will do the job best.

Split each fig in half horizontally and lay them flat on a plate. Scatter on some fennel seeds and toasted sliced almonds, and serve with coffee and Calvados.

A WORD ABOUT CANNED FIGS

Along with chickpeas and sardines, figs emerge from a can little the worse for their trauma. If you serve them very, very cold they can be really quite good. Just try not to think of fresh figs when you eat them.

FIGS WITH PERNOD

Tip a little Pernod, or Ricard, into the sticky syrup while the figs are being served. You will need no more than a few drops. A little Pernod goes a long way.

FIGUES FLAMBÉES

Or flaming figs. Drain the figs of their syrup. (This is not the infamous syrup of figs.) Tip the fruit into a hot frying pan, let it sizzle for a couple of minutes, and then pour over a small glass of liqueur (a liqueur glass if you have such a thing). Use whichever liqueur takes your fancy, or more likely whichever bottle is open. Try a mixture of Grand Marnier and brandy, or perhaps Kirsch (make it a good one—poor Kirsch tastes like lighter fuel to me). You will need a small glass for every two figs.

Strike a match, then set fire to the liquid (but not the kitchen). Turn the figs over with a fork to impregnate the fruit with the booze. Take care not to burn yourself. Douse the flames with a little cream, allow to bubble once or twice, and serve.

THE CRISP *see also page 85*

If we are going to be strict about timing, then the crisp, or its English cousin the crumble, doesn't really belong in this book. But the method is so absurdly simple and the dessert needs so little attention while cooking that I include it without apology.

In its simplest form it contains flour, butter, fruit, and sugar, the chemistry of which magically produces comfort food of the first order. Popular additions, such as almonds or oats to the crisp topping or alcohol or extra sugar to the fruit, are I think acceptable where they do not confuse the issue. Ground almonds, just a few rubbed in with the butter and flour, are a fine idea, though I think wholewheat flour and dark brown sugar ruin the flavor of both fruit and topping.

It was Fay Maschler, restaurant critic of London's *Evening Standard* newspaper, who said, in a review of one grand old hotel's restaurant, that the "apple crumble lacked the moment when the juices surge up and caramelize the crumbs." Here, I think, she identified the precise point at which this homey dish becomes a success. It is not always easy to achieve, but is quite crucial.

Plums, particularly greengages, produce the finest crisps for me. The extra juice they carry seems to do the trick, and their season is short enough not to allow me to tire of them. Rhubarb is another favorite. Damson plum crisp is absolute bliss. I will admit to rating few gastronomic pleasures higher than finding a bowl of cold fruit crisp in the refrigerator, and also to thinking the soggy bit between the fruit and the crisp topping the best bit of all.

PLUM CRISP

If the plums you have are not as ripe as they could be but plum crisp it must be, then stew the fruit until tender for 5 minutes or so with a couple of tablespoons of sugar and water before hiding them and the juice they exude under the topping. I have never found this necessary with really ripe fruit. The point of sprinkling water over the crisp mix before it meets the fruit is to allow some of the crumbs to stick together, giving a texture that is pebble-like rather than powdery.

FOR 4, GENEROUSLY

2 pounds ripe, juicy plums
sugar, to taste (probably
    about ¼ cup)
¾ cup all-purpose flour

⅔ cup ground almonds
½ cup butter
6 tablespoons granulated or
    light brown sugar

Cut the plums in half and remove the pits. Place them in a large, shallow baking dish. Sprinkle the fruit with as much sugar as you like. (I should have suggested you taste the plums first to ascertain their sweetness.)

If you have a food processor, whizz the flour, almonds, and butter for a few seconds until they resemble coarse bread crumbs. Stir in the sugar. Sprinkle the mixture with a tablespoon of cold water, and stir very lightly with a fork. Some of the crumbs should stick together, but be careful not to over mix. No food processor? Then rub the butter into the flour and almonds with your fingertips, and stir in the sugar. This will take about 5 minutes.

Scatter the topping over the fruit and bake in a preheated 400°F oven for about 35 minutes, until the top is crisp and golden and some of the juices from the fruit have bubbled up through the topping.

APRICOT-AMARETTI CRISP

FOR 4

2 pounds ripe apricots
a little sugar
8 amaretti cookies

¾ cup all-purpose flour
6 tablespoons butter
¼ cup sugar

Pull the apricots apart and remove the pits. Place the fruit in a shallow baking dish and sprinkle them with as much sugar as you would like—I suggest about 2 or 3 tablespoons—and 2 tablespoons of water.

Crush the cookies, not too finely, in their wrappers or in a paper bag with a rolling pin. Remember, if you buy them like this, there are two cookies in each tissue wrapping. Mix with the flour, then whizz in a food processor for a few seconds with the butter. Stir in the ¼ cup of sugar. Sprinkle a tablespoon of water over the mixture (see recipe opposite), then mix lightly with a fork.

Tip the mixture over the apricots, then bake in a preheated 400°F oven till golden, about 30 minutes.

➤ Accompany with almond cream, which is crushed *amaretti* cookies folded into softly whipped cream

Blackberry and Apple Crumble

An English classic. The apples are precooked for 5 minutes or so to give a fluffy texture that I appreciate in a dessert of this sort.

FOR 4

1 pound tart baking apples	*¾ cup all-purpose flour*
a little sugar	*¾ cup butter*
1 pound blackberries	*⅔ cup rolled oats*
(3 heaped cups)	*⅔ cup demerara sugar*

Wipe the apples and cut them in quarters, then remove the cores and slice each piece in two. Put them in a pan. Taste a slice for sweetness, and add a sprinkling of sugar accordingly. Add a tablespoon of water and cook over medium heat for about 5 minutes, until the apples start to soften. Throw in the blackberries and transfer to a shallow baking dish.

Whizz the flour and butter in the food processor for a few seconds till the mixture looks like crumbs. Stir in the oats and the brown sugar and scatter the mixture over the cooked apples and blackberries. Bake in a preheated 400°F oven for 30 minutes, or until crisp on top. Serve with cream.

Gooseberry Crisp

Gooseberries are perfect fruit for crisps, baking down to a wonderfully fragrant, soft green slush underneath the crispy, buttery topping. I am not sure that they benefit from any addition, either to topping or fruit. The simplest crisp, made from flour, butter, and sugar, is more suitable here than one with oats, almonds, or whatever. A fine dessert to be eaten with cold, thick cream.

FOR 4

1½ pounds gooseberries	*¾ cup butter*
sugar	*½ cup sugar*
1¼ cups all-purpose flour	

Pull off the worst of the stems and the largest of the dried flowers from the gooseberries. It shouldn't take long. Place them in a shallow dish (I use a 10-inch gratin dish) and toss gently with plenty of sugar. The amount you need depends on the tartness of the gooseberries, but they will probably need about 6 tablespoons.

Whizz the flour and butter in the food processor until it looks like coarse bread crumbs—a matter of seconds. Stir in the ½ cup of sugar, sprinkle a little water over, and shake the mixture or mix it gently with a fork till it resembles small pebbles. Tip the mixture on top of the fruit. Bake in a preheated 400°F oven for 30 minutes, then turn the heat up to 425°F until the top is golden and the gooseberry juices hopefully bubble up through the crisp topping.

Embellishments for Crisps

Although I like a straightforward flour-butter-sugar topping for gooseberries and rhubarb, I happily make additions to the basic mix if I think it will improve the dish.

Ground Almonds
Substitute them for some of the flour, using a quarter to a third of the quantity of flour called for. Best with fruits such as plums.

Amaretti Cookies
Continuing the almond theme, crush them to a coarse powder and either add to the flour or sprinkle on top of the finished dessert before baking. Very flattering to peaches and apricots.

Walnuts
Add just a handful of walnuts to the flour and butter as you whizz it, or crush them not too finely and scatter over the top. Best with apple and pear crisps. Serve a drizzle of maple syrup with the cream.

Oats
Go easy on these as they are inclined to turn the crisp into something rather too earthy-tasting. Substitute ⅓-⅔ cup oats for up to ⅓ cup flour. Avoid the temptation to use them with wholewheat flour unless you want to end up with a healthfood-restaurant-cardboard dessert.

Spices
Cinnamon works beautifully with apple and pear, nutmeg too, while coriander will lift a peach or blackberry crisp. A few fennel seeds will do wonders for a fig or apple mixture, though ground cloves will jolt your beautiful dessert into a reminder of a childhood toothache remedy.

Grated Orange or Lemon Zest
This should be added to the fruit rather than the topping, while sesame seeds and chopped pistachios and almonds can be sprinkled on top. If they are starting to brown too quickly, turn the heat down a fraction and suffer a few minutes more cooking time.

CONTEMPORARY CRISPS

➤ **The Mincemeat** one on page 84

➤ **Blueberry.** Add a mint leaf or two to the fruit and don't precook it

➤ **Peach and Almond.** Use those small peaches that invariably fail to ripen. Put ground almonds in the crisp topping and a few sliced ones on top

➤ **Damson and Gin.** Scatter classic crisp topping over the compote on page 29, saving some of the juice for pouring over at the table

➤ **Cherry and Almond.** Use fresh cherries, and don't pit them unless you have time to kill; toss the fruit with a little butter and sugar first. Use the almond crisp topping in the apricot recipe on page 60

➤ **Dried Fruit Salad.** Yesterday's dried fruit salad, with some of its juices and a spoonful of brandy, has worked well on several occasions in this house

scrambled eggs. Do not answer the phone, or pour yourself a drink unless it is from the Marsala bottle, and do not try to clear away the main-course dishes. Just beat.

When the mixture is thick and frothy—it should virtually stand in peaks—it is ready. Ladle the *zabaglione* into glasses and serve immediately while it is still warm and sensual.

A Few Good Things to Stir, Sprinkle, or Dunk into a Classic Zabaglione

➤ Vanilla: use pure vanilla extract and beat it in after all the other ingredients have started to thicken

➤ Cinnamon: either add a little ground spice to the mixture as it is thickening, or sprinkle some over the top

➤ Chocolate: just as the mixture finishes thickening, stir in a handful of chocolate, shaved with the help of a vegetable peeler from a dark and bittersweet block

➤ Italian *biscotti*, especially the hard ones with almonds embedded in them, are the best for *zabaglione*-dunking. British Rich Tea fingers aren't bad either

➤ Whipped cream: fold in softly whipped cream (you will need ½ cup of whipping cream to 4 egg yolks) to give a rich, thick dessert suitable for serving cold, or just tepid if you cannot wait

Banana Zabaglione

This is another version of my favorite pudding, bananas and custard.

FOR 6
the egg yolk, sugar and sweet
wine quantities opposite,
plus 2 ripe bananas

Make the *zabaglione* as opposite. While it is still warm stir in the bananas, sliced as thinly as half-dollars. Serve in glasses and eat while still warm.

Strawberry *Zabaglione*

To the classic recipe above add a handful or two of sliced ripe strawberries. A nice almondy cookie would go down well too, I expect.

Zabaglione with Black-Currant Purée

FOR 6

½ pound frozen
   black currants
½ cup + 1 tablespoon sugar

4 eggs yolks
½ cup Marsala or
   other sweet white wine

Put the black currants in a pan with the 1 tablespoon of sugar and a tablespoon of water. Cook over medium heat till the fruit bursts and a thick purple syrup forms, about 5 or 6 minutes.

Put the yolks, ½ cup of sugar, and sweet wine in a bowl over a pan of simmering water and beat till thick with an electric mixer. Expect this to take about 10-15 minutes. Remove from the heat.

Spoon 2 tablespoons of the fruit and its juice into each of six glasses and fill with spoonfuls of *zabaglione*. Eat with a teaspoon, marbling the rich purple juice and golden custard as you eat.

The Twenty-minute *Tiramisu*

Tiramisu is that creamy, alcoholic mess of sponge cake and cream cheese—sort of Italian trifle. No longer quite so hip, it is seen less on menus, so addicts must make it themselves. Traditionally, it is prepared the night before so that the sponge will soak up the liquid and the cream cheese topping thickens somewhat. I will not argue with the importance of this, but, for addicts such as myself, this quick version is not so very far away from the real thing.

FOR 4 (OR 2 ADDICTS)

20 ladyfingers
¾ cup very strong
  coffee, preferably espresso
7 tablespoons Marsala or, if
  you must, sweet honey
4 eggs

⅓ cup sugar
1 pound mascarpone cheese
1 ounce bittersweet chocolate,
  grated, or 2 tablespoons
  unsweetened cocoa powder

Break up the ladyfingers into short lengths and drop them into a shallow serving dish. Mix the coffee and the Marsala and pour it over the cookies. Press them down into the liquid; they must soak it all up.

Separate the eggs: yolks in one large bowl, whites in another. Beat the egg yolks and the sugar with an electric mixer, then mix in the mascarpone. Wash the beaters, then beat the egg whites till stiff. Scoop them into the mascarpone and mix thoroughly with a metal spoon. Spoon the mascarpone mixture over the softened ladyfingers. Spread reasonably flat, then sprinkle the chocolate or cocoa powder over.

Leave for as long as you can before serving; even 10 minutes in the refrigerator will help.

Sweet Soufflé Omelet

If you have an egg in the refrigerator and a spoonful of preserves in the bottom of the jar, then you have a dessert. I would not suggest cooking more than one of these at once as they are best eaten within seconds of leaving the pan. After a reasonably substantial supper one omelet will probably serve two. Probably the best I have ever eaten was when I had some cold poached rhubarb to fill it with.

MAKES 1

3 eggs, separated
1 heaped tablespoon sugar

1 tablespoon butter

Put the egg yolks into a mixing bowl with the sugar and beat until thick—a matter of seconds with an electric mixer, a little longer by hand. Beat the egg whites into stiff peaks and fold into the egg yolk and sugar with a metal spoon or spatula.

Melt the butter in your trusty omelet pan, the one that doesn't stick, and when it starts to fizz swoosh in the egg mixture. Cook over medium heat until set on the underside, then either put it under a preheated broiler to cook the top a little or into a hot oven (the broiler will be quicker and take only a few seconds). Add the filling of your choice (see below) and fold the omelet in half. Slide it out of the pan—it may need a good shove with a spatula—and eat while hot and fluffy.

Good Things to Put in Your Sweet Omelet

➤ A good sprinkling of sugar, perhaps flavored with vanilla

➤ Warmed cherry preserves, the sharpish Morello variety rather than the bubblegum-black-cherry one. You will need 2 or 3 heaped tablespoons per omelet

➤ Crushed red berries tarted up with a glug from the *crème de cassis* bottle

➤ Apple slices, fried in a little butter and sugar till golden, sprinkled with a few anise seeds

The Crêpe *see also page 40*

The French don't eat crêpes from street stalls, I have been told; only tourists do. And yet the best ones I have come across were in Paris, tucked behind the Rue Mouffetard street market, where the sidewalk was congested with French students eating golden crêpes from white paper. Perhaps the person who told me thinks that the British no longer eat fish and chips in the street either. He should come to north London on a Friday night.

Made at home, crêpes are one of the quickest hot desserts if you do nothing fancy with them. They are not difffcult if you get the batter right and have a pan you can trust, though your first one or two may glue themselves to it. These crêpes are the cook's perk, incidentally, to be wolfed while you attempt a third.

Sophie Grigson went into great detail about making crêpes one Saturday in her compulsive column in *The Independent* newspaper. The recipe below is hers, and is the best I have come across for thin, French crêpes. They also taste of something, which is more than you can say for most. I have parted company with her when it comes to resting the batter, my impatience getting the better of me.

THIN FRENCH CRÊPES

MAKES 10 CRÊPES/FOR 3-4

4 tablespoons butter
¾ cup all-purpose flour
pinch of salt
1 tablespoon sugar
1 extra large egg, lightly beaten
1 egg yolk

1½ cups milk
1½ tablespoons brandy
2 teaspoons orange-flower
   water
butter, for greasing

Melt the butter in a small pan, remove from the heat, and pour into a cup to cool. (It will take an age to cool in the hot pan.) Sift the flour with the salt. Mix in the sugar. Make a well in the center and add the egg and egg yolk, plus the melted butter, which should have cooled a bit by now.

Start stirring, gradually drawing in the flour, and adding the milk to give a smooth batter. Stir in the brandy and flower water.

This is where Sophie rests her batter, so that the "starch will be almost completely gelatinized, and the batter will be able to carry a greater quantity of liquid. That means you can thin it a little more to make lighter crêpes." The words that caught my eye, though, were: "As soon as the batter is made up, the starch in the flour begins to swell, which means you can use it straight away."

Cooking the Crêpes

Brush a heavy-based frying pan, or crêpe pan if you have such a thing, with a little butter. (My own small crêpe pan now has such a well-established nonstick layer built up on it that I can put it in the dishwasher and it still doesn't stick.) Put it over medium heat until the butter melts and breaks out into tiny bubbles.

Pour in a ladleful of batter, then swirl it around the pan by rolling the pan from side to side until the bottom is covered in a thin layer. Pour any extra batter back into the bowl. Place over the heat and cook for a minute or so before lifting the edge of the crêpe from the pan with a metal spatula and peeping to see if the underside is golden brown in patches. If it is, loosen the crêpe with the spatula, then lift it over onto the other side. This will take less time to cook. Turn the cooked crêpe onto a plate and carry on till you have ten crêpes.

Seven Good Things to do with a Crêpe

➤ **Citrus juices:** mix freshly squeezed lemon, orange, and lime juices and sweeten with a little liquid honey (you won't need very much). Drizzle them over the crêpes while still hot

➤ **Spiced butters:** soften some unsalted butter in a small pan, then spike with sweet spices, freshly ground if possible. Suitable contenders are cinnamon, cardamom, and nutmeg

➤ **Flower waters:** sprinkle each hot crêpe with orange-flower or rosewater, dress with a dash of fresh orange juice, and eat while hot

➤ **Apple purée:** spread with liberal quantities of rough apple purée (see page 36)

➤ **Melted chocolate:** use rich bittersweet chocolate, softened in a bowl

➤ **Honey and nuts:** liquid honey is best if you don't want to tear your crêpe to shreds. Nuts should be broken up a little and toasted till golden and fragrant

➤ **Squeeze of lemon:** you can't beat a squeeze of fresh lemon juice. And that doesn't mean the stuff in the plastic yellow lemon or a bottle

Clafoutis

You can't cook a clafoutis in half-an-hour, but so absurdly simple is the method (whizz it up, pour it in a pan, and bake it) that I include it here in the hope that you can prepare the rest of the meal while the clafoutis cooks.

Clafoutis is little more than a sweet version of popovers or Yorkshire pudding, usually dotted with cherries or apples. It is another one on the list for those who, if they are to eat desserts at all, want them to be hot, traditional, and substantial.

FOR 4

4 eggs	*6 tablespoons sugar*
½ cup + 1 tablespoon	*1 cup whipping cream*
all-purpose flour	*1 cup whole milk*
large pinch of salt	*fruit of your choice, see below*

Butter a 10-inch tart pan or baking pan. Whizz all the ingredients, apart from the fruit, in the blender or food processor, or beat them all together with a balloon whisk.

Put the fruit in the bottom of the pan, pour the batter over and bake in a preheated 400°F oven. It is done when well-risen, golden, and firm, probably about 40 minutes. Sprinkle with sugar before eating.

Pear Clafoutis

Peel, slice, and core 1 pound ripe pears. Toss the slices in a little *eau de vie* before putting them in the buttered pan.

Cherry Clafoutis

The classic fruit to use in this batter pudding. You will need 1 pound cherries for a 4-egg clafoutis. Bottled red cherries, particularly those in brandy, are especially good here.

Fig Clafoutis

Slice 6 figs in half through the stem. Roll each half in liquid honey, then put in the buttered pan.

Prune Clafoutis

Soaked prunes or the very soft French ones, rolled in brandy, make one of the best-flavored fillings. Scatter a few sliced almonds over the top just before baking. Serve warm with sugar and cream. You will need about ¾ pound (2 cups) pitted prunes, which is 1 pound before pitting.

➤ A glass of brandy of some sort or another works well with a hot, sugary batter pudding. Calvados would be my choice, though almost anything would be suitable

PINEAPPLES

The less you do to pineapple the better. A little alcohol, in the form of Kirsch or Cointreau, or perhaps rum, or a companionable fruit such as passion fruit or orange, is all I will offer here. A truly ripe pineapple needs no embellishment.

Choose a pineapple that is heavy for its size. It should have a noticeable pineapple smell that should hit you from several inches away. To check for ripeness pull a leaf from its crown. If it comes out easily then the fruit is ripe; if not, put it back for another day.

In theory the core is indigestible and is usually removed. I rarely do so. If the fruit is deeply ripe then the core will be perfectly edible, though it may have a little more crispness to it. The real point of a pineapple is its juice. It must be sweet and copious. You must choose your fruit very carefully.

You can find pineapples in good condition from late autumn till May or June. They seem to lose their real magic only in high summer. But there is enough other fruit around at that time anyway. Pineapples are at their best when there is little else around, making them twice as welcome as they would be in the summer. Much of the fruit we see in the markets comes from Hawaii or the West Indies, and very good it is too.

Lately there has been an influx of miniature pineapples. They are easier to carry home, though slightly more expensive. These little fruit never seem to achieve the same heaviness of perfume and juiciness of flesh of their more majestic sisters. I do, though, find them ideal for one person—a large fruit can last just that bit too long if you are devouring it by yourself. Mind you, it will keep, cut side covered with plastic wrap, in the refrigerator for a day or two.

The Canned Stuff

Some people swear by canned pineapple. I am not sure I agree. It is such a pale shadow of the fresh fruit, and somehow so limp and flaccid. For emergencies only, though I will concede it is a more successful candidate for canning than the strawberry. But then, isn't everything?

ANANAS AU KIRSCH

The epitome of the Parisian bistro dessert. A joy when the fruit is perfectly ripe and the *eau de vie* is one of the finest. I have tasted this treatment of pineapple quite recently in a boisterous bistro close to a favorite building of mine, the Institut du Monde Arabe in Paris, the exact location of which has disappeared in a fog of Fleurie. I will find it again, though. The pineapple was sublime, even if it was only a taster from a friend's plate. I had succumbed to something altogether more hedonistic—icebergs of poached meringue floating in a dish of vanilla-scented custard.

FOR 4, AT LEAST

1 medium pineapple,   *2 tablespoons Kirsch*
    absolutely ripe (see page 104)

Peel the pineapple if you wish, though the skin is easy enough to remove as you eat. Slice the pineapple in thick slices, almost, I suggest, 1 inch thick. Put two slices, a large and a small one, on each plate. Upend the Kirsch over the fruit and leave for 10 minutes or so before eating.

➤   If the pineapple is not quite as juicy as you would wish it to be, then sprinkle a little sugar over it after adding the Kirsch

➤   Cointreau, the orange-based liqueur, can be used instead of Kirsch, as can rum, for those who like the stuff

BANANAS *see also pages 73, 75, 95, 97, 171*

Bananas are a trusty friend to the short-of-time cook. Reliable, ubiquitous, cheap, and satisfying, this is one fruit that never lets you down. It is simple to gauge ripeness and quality just by looking at the skin. I prefer a slightly underripe banana for eating and cooking, so I tend to gravitate toward long, perfect specimens with little or no brown markings and green tinges at the stem ends. Banana connoisseurs are more likely to head for brown-freckled ones, whose skins feel thinner and have no green about them. They will be sweeter this way, and the flavor will be deeper.

It is very easy to take bananas for granted. Any market will offer a hand of the fruit in one condition or another. Rarely are they disappointing. Bananas hate the cold and in deepest winter they may suffer from too cold a storage temperature and be slightly gray inside, but this can be detected too by a slight gray tone to the yellow skin. Store your fruit in the refrigerator and it will turn black on you. Banana experts say that spring is the best time for quality, though I find them one of the more trustworthy fruits all year round.

As effortless desserts go, the banana takes some beating. Broiled or baked, without even so much as peeling, you will get a rich, creamy result in 20 minutes or so. Eaten hot from the oven, only a pitcher of cream or the flesh from a passion fruit will be needed to turn such simplicity into a memorable dessert. Sliced raw into thick yogurt and stirred with flower honey, the banana offers an ending to a meal that will please even the most neurotic of healthy eaters. Broiled with citrus juice and spices, it will placate the most hedonistic, while simply peeled and eaten on the run, monkey-style, it should please everyone but the pretentious.

Friends of the banana include cream in all its forms, thick yogurt, citrus fruits, particularly lime, and spices such as cardamom and nutmeg. I am far from convinced about chocolate and bananas, though I am assured that sliced banana with hot chocolate sauce can be heavenly. But then, is there anything that could better a properly made banana custard? I think not.

BAKED BANANAS

Bake unpeeled fruit in a preheated 350°F oven till the skins are black and soft, about 25 minutes. Split the skins and pour a little cream inside. Eat the cold cream and the hot bananas from their jackets with a teaspoon.

BAKED BANANA WITH CARDAMOM AND ORANGE

FOR 4

4 ripe bananas, peeled   *2 cardamom pods*
⅓-½ cup brown sugar   *juice of 1 large orange*
4 tablespoons butter

Cut the bananas in slices about ½ inch thick. Put them into a baking dish, sprinkle with sugar, and dot the butter, in little pieces, on top.

Bake the bananas for 7-8 minutes, depending on their ripeness, in a preheated 400°F oven. While the bananas are baking, remove the little black cardamom seeds from their husks and crush them roughly. If you do not have a pestle and mortar, then put them in a paper bag and bash them gently with the end of a rolling pin.

When the bananas are hot and have softened somewhat, take them out of the oven, scatter with the crushed cardamom, and sprinkle the orange juice over. Return to the oven for 1 minute. Serve immediately.

BROILED BANANAS

Lynda Brown, the gardener-cook, shares my passion for bananas. She broils hers unpeeled, no doubt in an attempt to contain all their sweet goodness.

"Place your banana, unpeeled, on a pan or in a fireproof dish and grill under a hot broiler for about 7-10 minutes, during which the skin will blacken and the juice ooze out to form its own delicious sauce. Tear off a strip of the skin and eat the flesh with a spoon, not forgetting to scrape up all the sauce."

➤ See also banana custard, page 95

HOT BANANA BRIOCHE

Yogurt would be my immediate choice to lubricate this favorite fruit toast, but I have been known to go quite over the top and serve it with banana custard.

FOR 4

4 slices of brioche or　　　　　　*4 ripe bananas, peeled*
　panettone, ½ inch thick　　　*juice of ½ orange*
rum, which is quite optional　　*thick plain yogurt, to serve*

Preheat the broiler until it is very hot. Put the slices of brioche or *panettone* on the broiler pan. Sprinkle with rum if you wish. Slice the bananas as thick as half-dollars and lay them, slightly overlapping, on top of the bread.

Squeeze the orange juice over and place the bread under the broiler, until the banana starts to turn golden brown, about 5-7 minutes. Serve hot with thick yogurt.

FOIL-BAKED BANANAS WITH APRICOT SAUCE

FOR 4

4 ripe bananas, peeled　　　　*a 16-ounce can apricots*

You will need 4 pieces of foil, each large enough to be folded around a banana.

Place the foil on the work surface. Place a banana on each one, then bring up the sides of the foil to make little packets for the fruit. Whizz the apricots to a purée in a blender or processor with a little of their canning syrup.

Spoon the purée into the little packets and seal thoroughly by scrunching together the foil along the top. Bake in a preheated 400°F oven for about 20 minutes. (Open one slightly and test the fruit with a skewer.) Serve hot, and let everyone open up their own packet, which will be full of fruit-scented steam.

BROILED BANANAS WITH CITRUS AND SPICES

I can't remember exactly where this recipe came from or why it is in my tatty, handwritten cookbook. It originally had cardamom in it too, but on trying it again I felt something had to go. It could have been either of the other spices.

FOR 4

4 large, firm bananas	*a pinch of ground coriander*
juice of 1 lime	*3 tablespoons butter*
¼ cup orange juice	*confectioners' sugar*
a pinch of ground nutmeg	*2 tablespoons sliced almonds*

Peel the bananas and cut them in half lengthwise. Put them in a shallow ovenproof dish, or on a baking sheet, flat side up. Mix together the juices and spoon them over the bananas. Mix the spices with the butter and place blobs of it over the fruit.

Cook under a preheated broiler till the bananas are golden and tender, about 6 minutes. Pull the dish out from the heat, dust with confectioners' sugar, and scatter over the sliced almonds. Put back under the broiler till slightly browned. Eat warm.

Hot Banana Pudding

An unusual sounding method with a pleasing, almost soufflé-like result, though the color is not as pretty as it could be— unless you are particularly fond of beige. It is just the thing for a chilly March evening, and most of the ingredients will probably be on hand anyway.

FOR 2, GENEROUSLY

½ cup whipping cream	*3 very ripe bananas, whizzed*
½ vanilla bean or 1 teaspoon	*to a smooth pulp*
vanilla extract	*3 extra large egg whites*
¼ cup sugar ⎤ beaten till	*2 teaspoons lemon juice*
3 extra large egg yolks ⎦ thick and creamy	

Whip the cream until thick and creamy. It should be sloppy, not yet capable of standing in peaks. Slit the vanilla bean in half and scrape the little black seeds into the cream, or add the vanilla extract. Mix well, then fold into the cream with the egg yolk and sugar mixture and the pulped bananas. Continue beating till thick and creamy—a matter of seconds with an electric mixer.

Butter a 6-inch soufflé dish or similar ovenproof dish and sprinkle a little sugar over it. Beat the egg whites till they stand in stiff peaks, then fold them gently and thoroughly into the banana cream. Stir in the lemon juice. Scoop the mixture gently into the buttered dish and bake in a preheated 350°F oven till puffed and risen, about 20 minutes or so. The outside should be golden brown and risen almost to the rim of the dish, the inside creamy and scented with banana and vanilla.

BANANAS WITH BUTTER AND BROWN SUGAR

Bananas are sweet enough, and rarely need sugar. But when baked in this manner, with lime juice (you can use a lemon if that is what you have) and butter, they take on a velvety consistency and a rich flavor.

FOR 4

butter, somewhere between
  2 and 4 tablespoons
4 large, ripe but firm bananas

3 heaped tablespoons soft
  brown sugar
juice of 1 lime or ½ lemon

Butter a shallow baking dish. Peel the bananas and cut them in half lengthwise. Squeeze them into the dish; they should nestle up to one another. Dot a little more butter over the fruit, then sprinkle with brown sugar. Squeeze the lime juice over and bake for 15 minutes, maybe a bit longer, in a preheated 350°F oven. Serve with cream.

BANANA-YOGURT FOOL

FOR 2

4 soft, ripe bananas
  peeled

1¼ cups thick, creamy,
  plain yogurt

Drop the bananas in the blender and whizz till smooth, but stop before they turn gummy. Add a spoonful of yogurt if they refuse to move, or use a food processor. Scrape into a bowl with a rubber spatula and fold in the remaining yogurt, which should be chilled and thick. Spoon into wineglasses and chill till you are ready to eat.

Bananas with Cream and Kirsch

As always, omit the vanilla if the stuff you have is flavoring rather than true vanilla extract.

FOR 2

2 large, ripe bananas	*2 teaspoons Kirsch*
lemon juice	*½ teaspoon vanilla extract*
⅓ cup whipping cream	

Peel the bananas and slice them thickly. Put them in a bowl with a sprinkling of lemon juice. Whip the cream lightly so that it still has a pourable consistency, and stir in the Kirsch and vanilla. Scrape the cream into the dish with the bananas, and toss very gently so as not to damage the fruit. Spoon into glasses and serve—with a crisp almondy cookie perhaps.

Blueberry and Banana Salad

Slice a few bananas, add in a handful of blueberries, and squirt a little lemon juice over. Eat immediately.

Creams and Cream Cheeses

I am not a fan of those cheeses labeled cream cheese. I list below other possibilities, altogether more interesting.

Mascarpone *see also pages 47, 56-57, 163, 166*
Cream cheese for me used to mean a rather yellow, bland, and crumbly curd cheese sold from large tubs. Invariably used for cheesecakes, it had a faintly sour taste—I suspect because the demand was low. Failing that there were foil packages of bland and crumbly white paste, equally nasty and hideously expensive to boot.

Enter mascarpone. This Italian immigrant from Lombardy has transformed the cream-cheese market overnight. It has a rich, firm consistency and a certain voluptuousness. Sweet and mild, it is interesting enough to eat by the spoonful, straight from the tub. On a midnight refrigerator-raid I have been known to eat alternate spoonfuls with apricot preserves; at teatime it is a luxurious spread for English muffins and toast, and even more special when topped with a handful of strawberries that have been sprinkled with balsamic vinegar.

It is somewhat expensive, though tempered by the fact that a little goes a long way.

Ricotta *see also pages 130, 167*
This is a fresh Italian cheese of which I am becoming enormously fond. I include it here on the grounds that it is a friend to the quick cook and can provide an instant dessert when served alongside perfectly ripe greengage plums, apricots, and figs. One of the most versatile of cheeses, it can be whizzed into cream puddings to be flavored with brandy or rum, stirred through with chopped candied peel or dark chocolate chips. Use within a couple of days of purchase because it does not keep well. Left carelessly wrapped (here speaks the voice of experience again) it will pick up every flavor in the refrigerator. It also has the advantage of being the cheapest of these cheeses.

Fromage Blanc
This can be substituted in many of the recipes where mascarpone is mentioned. It stars as an essential ingredient in fools and fruit desserts, and as such it is hard to beat, offering the creaminess of its high-fat sisters without the richness. In its purest form a fresh curd cheese, it is more often than not mixed with cream, resulting in a thicker, richer, and more delectable cheese. Most supermarkets offer tubs of *fromage blanc* with their fat percentage clearly marked. The lowfat ones are softer and, to my mind, less interesting. In summer an instant pudding can be made by serving a little bowl of *fromage blanc* topped with finely chopped flesh from a melon or puréed berries. A sprig of mint or even a little flower would be quite harmonious with such a delicate, summery pot.

Lowfat Products
A word about products labeled lowfat or light or "lite." Generally speaking and without getting boringly technical, these products are the basic high-fat version made lighter with the addition of air and water. Of course, a pot of cream cheese will be lighter in fat if a third of the tub is nothing more than

air; it's what gives "lite" products their characteristic whipped texture. There are some very well-known corporate giants whose food empires are built on little more than air, water, and hype. Interestingly, the French, who embraced the lowfat dairy product like a nation possessed, have recently lost interest in such stuff in favor of the real thing, with lowfat foods dropping to some 2 percent of the market. And they can still boast one of the lowest rates of cardiac arrest in the world. Or so I am told.

Crema alla Mascarpone

A somewhat addictive and slightly alcoholic cream, this is only fractionally more effort than one of those instant pudding things.

FOR 4

2 eggs, separated	1 tablespoon brandy or
¼ cup sugar	Kirsch
1¼ cups mascarpone cheese	

Cream the egg yolks with the sugar for a few seconds, then add the mascarpone and beat till light and creamy—a matter of minutes with an electric mixer. Stir in the brandy or Kirsch.

Wash the beaters, then beat the egg whites till stiff. Fold them into the cream, gently but thoroughly, using a metal spoon. Spoon into glasses and chill for as long as you can, 20 minutes at the least. The cream will thicken slightly.

MASCARPONE WITH PRUNES AND ALMONDS

Prunes and cream cheese are a classic combination. They usually manifest themselves as prunes stuffed with cottage cheese, which is fine, but a better variation to my mind is mascarpone cheese served with a prune purée. I have seen jars of the purée but not often enough to include in a recipe, so suggest that you make your own with either prunes soaked in brandy or those plump and moist fruits from Agen in France. They are not so hard to find nowadays.

FOR 4

*½ pound prunes soaked in
brandy
1 tablespoon apple juice or
water, if necessary*

*¾ cup mascarpone cheese
12 whole almonds*

Cut the prunes in half and remove the pits. Liquidize the fruit in a blender, adding 1 tablespoon of apple juice or water if it seems rather dry. The consistency needs to be that of a thick purée. Place scoops of mascarpone on each of four small plates, then spoon some of the purée onto each one. Split each almond into approximately four slivers and scatter them over the cheese and purée.

GINGERED RICOTTA

Golden, translucent pieces of stem ginger in syrup are a useful delicacy to have in the cupboard. Here they add a somewhat luxurious element to a simple mixture of lowfat cream cheeses and almonds.

FOR 2

*½ cup ricotta cheese
⅓ cup fromage blanc
1 tablespoon sugar
2 tablespoons ground
almonds*

*2 lumps of preserved stem
ginger in syrup
2 tablespoons syrup from the
ginger jar
brandy snaps, to serve*

Push the ricotta through a strainer with a wooden spoon and stir in the *fromage blanc*. Stir in the sugar and almonds. Cut the lumps of ginger in small dice, then stir into the ricotta with the syrup.

Chill for at least 20 minutes so that the flavors blend, then serve in tiny pots with brandy snaps to dip.

Fresh Fromage Blanc

This is a lovely, softly piquant cream of which I am particularly fond. Its soft consistency and gentle tartness could not be more flattering to fruits (I am thinking of summer berries here), though I am happy enough to indulge in a whole small bowl of it all to myself.

FOR 4

1 cup thick plain yogurt   *3 egg whites*
1 cup whipping cream

Put the yogurt, which must be drained of excess liquid, in a large bowl. In another one, whip the cream with a hand or electric mixer, until it forms soft peaks. It should not be too stiff. Fold the cream into the yogurt gently and thoroughly using a metal spoon. Beat the egg whites till stiff. Fold them into the cream and yogurt, then chill for 15 minutes. Serve in little pots or cups with a teaspoon.

➤ Grind a little nutmeg over the cream—a quite delightful addition

➤ Put a few dark berries, such as blackberries or loganberries, into a serving bowl. Crush them lightly with a fork till they bleed purple juice, then spoon some of the *fromage blanc* over. Stir gently, just enough to streak the cream with purple

➤ Serve in small bowls with a little (and I mean a little) demerara sugar

➤ Stir a little fruit preserves, apricot, quince, or fig perhaps, into the cheese. Eat piled onto little water biscuits

Staples and Stodge

A water biscuit and a slice of fruit is not my idea of heaven on a cold evening. I want something satisfying, comforting, and hot after my trudge home and quickly made pantry supper. Steaming bowls of sleep-inducing stodge is much more my style. Rice and cornmeal are the two staples I continually rely on for quick, hot puddings. They keep well in airtight jars, and are both frugal and satisfying in the extreme.

Don't believe anyone who tells you rice pudding isn't fast food. Creamy rice puddings scented in Middle-Eastern style with rosewater and spiked with pistachios are perhaps my favorite examples of sweet comfort food, and can be knocked together in no time at all. A bowl of *gnocchi*, sticky and golden and smelling softly of vanilla and lemon, is just as fast, and to me is the most welcome of all.

The Twenty-minute Rice Pudding

Here is a creamy rice pudding in less time than it takes to heat up a ready-made one. There are canned ones, of course, but the rice is too soft and pappy. Short-grain or *arborio* (risotto) rice is essential if the grains are to swell up in juicy fashion.

FOR 4

8 heaped tablespoons arborio
  or short-grain rice
1¼ cups milk
1¼ cups heavy cream
a vanilla bean, split in half
  lengthwise, or 1 teaspoon
  vanilla extract

6 tablespoons water
2 tablespoons butter
⅓-½ cup sugar

Put the rice in a medium-sized, heavy-based pan, then pour in the milk, cream, vanilla bean or extract, and water. Bring to a boil over medium heat, then turn down the flame until the milk is bubbling gently, just as you would have it for a risotto.

Let it cook for 15-20 minutes until the rice has swelled with the milk. It should be soft when done, but not without a little bite. Add the butter, whip out the vanilla bean, and stir in the sugar. As soon as the sugar has dissolved, the pudding is ready.

How to get a Crispy Skin on your Fast Rice Pudding

Connoisseurs of rice pudding demand a crisp skin that is golden brown all over. Rice-pudding-skin bores will also insist on a patch of dark brown skin that is swollen and on the verge of being charred.

After stirring in the sugar, scrape the pudding into a heat-proof serving dish. Get the broiler really hot, then place the pudding underneath, about 1 inch away from the heat.

Broil for 3 or 4 minutes, until the skin is golden brown in most parts, dark brown in others.

Rice Pudding with Rosewater, Cardamom, and Pistachio

A classic from Afghanistan, this I first encountered at Ruth and David Watson's pub, the Fox and Goose at Fressingfield in Suffolk, England. Known affectionately as the Effing G., this is one of those country pubs with good food and the sort of bar where you can doze off of an afternoon in a squashy chair. This is my version of their recipe, which is in turn a version of Jeremy Round's. They also make a mean onion *bhaji*, but that is another matter.

FOR 2

8 heaped tablespoons arborio
   or short-grain rice
1¼ cups milk
1¼ cups heavy cream
6 tablespoons water
*a vanilla bean, split in half
   lengthwise, or 1 teaspoon
   vanilla extract*

1 teaspoon cardamom pods
*2 handfuls of pistachio nuts
   in their shells*
⅓-½ cup sugar
4 teaspoons rosewater

Follow the recipe opposite with the rice, milk, cream, water, and vanilla. While the rice is cooking, remove the seeds from the cardamom pods and the shells from the pistachios. Grind the cardamom seeds to a powder in a spice mill or coffee grinder, or using a pestle and mortar. Chop the pistachios roughly.

Stir the sugar into the rice, and take out the vanilla bean if you used one, then add the ground cardamom. Stir in the rose-water. Cook for a further minute, then taste the pudding. Add more sugar—I think this dish should be really quite sweet—and more rosewater if you like. Serve while still warm and creamy, in two small bowls, with the chopped green pistachios scattered on top.

➤ I once added a few pieces of gold leaf to the last dish, just peeled from the backing paper in little bits and sprinkled over the pudding. It was an absolutely charming addition and, surprisingly, not as pretentious as you might expect. Gold leaf, in little books, is available from artists' suppliers and Indian grocers. And it is fearfully expensive

FIVE NICE RICE PUDDINGS

Cinnamon Rice Pudding
To the basic rice pudding recipe on page 116 (not the rosewater one), add a pinch or two of ground cinnamon and grate in a little nutmeg at the start of cooking.

Orange-Flower Water Rice Pudding
In the Middle East they are very fond, so I gather, of adding orange-blossom water to their sweet rice, in much the same way as in India they use rosewater. Follow either the basic rice pudding recipe or, even better, the scented one, adding orange-flower water in place of the rosewater.

Rice Pudding and Preserves
Forget school lunches. Sweet rice, thick and creamy, can be really good with a blob of decent preserves. The trick is not to be tempted to stir it in too thoroughly; just stir the preserves enough to streak the rice with purple or red rather than to turn it a monotone hideous pink. It is the subtlety of a mixed mouthful of tart preserves and unctuous creamy rice that is worth eating.

Best preserves for stirring into rice pudding are black currant, apricot, or rhubarb, because their slight tartness is more welcome swirled into the bland creamy mass than the ubiquitous sweet and sticky strawberry.

Saffron Rice Pudding
Add a couple of pinches of saffron powder with a little ground

cinnamon to the basic pudding recipe when you add the milk and cream to the rice. A squeeze of lemon at the end of cooking will not go amiss.

RICE PUDDING WITH ORANGE ZEST AND GINGER

My unauthentic version of an Iranian-style rice pudding.

FOR 2

1 small carrot, coarsely grated
grated zest of 1 small orange
2 heaped tablespoons golden raisins
2 heaped tablespoons sliced almonds

2 pieces of preserved stem ginger
*   in syrup*
a little syrup from the
*   ginger jar*

Make the rice pudding as in the basic recipe on page 116. Add the grated carrot, orange zest, and raisins when you add the sugar, then they will keep their sparkle. Toast the almonds till golden under the broiler or in a nonstick frying pan.

When the rice is cooked, divide it between two small dishes and scatter the toasted almonds on top. Chop the ginger in dice, add it in a small heap on top of the rice, and drizzle a little of the syrup over.

SWEET GNOCCHI

Sustaining, soothing, and mildly soporific, this is surely the most comforting pudding of all: the dessert-eater's answer to mashed potatoes or perhaps *aligot*. It will not amuse cake fanciers and their kind who would no doubt blanch if given a bowl of the sweet yellow mush, even if served piping hot and softly scented with lemon and vanilla.

The term *gnocchi* is confusing here; perhaps sweet polenta would have been more accurate. It may have helped convey the extraordinarily frugal and nannying quality of such a pudding. Whatever you call it, it is a quick, hot pudding made with sugar, fine cornmeal or rice flour, milk, and eggs. This is a simple dish that will be ruined by second-rate ingredients. Choose a fine cornmeal rather than the coarser varieties, which will give a grainy texture not wanted here. More than ever, it is essential to use the finest vanilla extract rather than the nasty flavorings around.

The recipe came to me via Matthew Fort, the Food Editor of the *Guardian* newspaper, who in turn procured it from Francesco Zanchetta, the chef at Riva in southwest London. Matthew serves it Riva style, that is, left to cool, then cut into shapes and baked with a honey and Marsala syrup (see page 121). I have stopped halfway through his recipe, and offer it as a rib-sticking golden mush for a chilly spring evening.

FOR 2

2 egg yolks	*grated zest of 1 small lemon*
¾ cup sugar	*(or ½ large one)*
¼ cup fine cornmeal	*vanilla extract*
or 3 tablespoons	*1¼ cups milk*

Beat the egg yolks and the sugar with a small whisk or electric mixer till light and creamy. Beat in the cornmeal or rice flour, grated lemon, and vanilla extract. Pour in the milk and continue beating or whisking till all is amalgamated. Check there are no lumps at the bottom of the bowl.

Pour into a medium-sized, heavy-based saucepan—nonstick would be good for this—and place over medium heat. Bring to a boil, stirring every few seconds or so, then turn down to a simmer. Keep stirring, almost continually now. It will suddenly change from a thin yellow liquid with lumps to a rich, thick custard. Continue stirring, paying special attention to the corners, for 3 minutes until it has thickened.

Divide between two small serving dishes, allow to cool very slightly, and eat while still warm.

➤ Spoon a gloop of liquid honey on top. Chestnut honey is the one I use. Partially stir it in as you eat

➤ Forget the "allow to cool very slightly" and eat it steaming hot, dipping each spoonful of pudding first into a dish of cold milk, then into the sugar bowl

➤ Open up that can of vacuum-packed chestnuts that has been sitting in the cupboard for weeks. Scatter the contents on a baking sheet and broil till sizzling. Chop coarsely, then stir into the golden mush

Gnocchi with Honey, Marsala, and Butter Sauce

This is my version of what I ate at Matthew Fort's, which is his version of what he ate at Riva.

Follow the previous recipe until it tells you to spoon the mixture into bowls. Don't do that. Scrape it out onto a buttered plate instead. Smooth it with the back of the spoon to a thickness of about ½ inch. Leave to cool. It won't take long, about 20 minutes.

Melt 2 tablespoons of liquid honey with 2 tablespoons of Marsala in a small saucepan over medium heat. Whisk in 2 tablespoons of cold butter and bring to a boil. Remove from the heat, and cover with a lid.

Cut the paste in square or diamond shapes, probably about eight to ten. With help from a metal spatula, lift them onto a very lightly buttered baking sheet. Brush with a small amount of melted butter and bake in a preheated 400°F oven for 8 minutes. They will be slightly puffed and soft to handle.

Take them out of the oven, scoop each one up carefully with a metal spatula, and arrange on two large plates. Pour the warm Marsala sauce over. Enough for two.

➤ A small ripe pear, peeled if you can be bothered, and sliced thinly, can be warmed through in the honey and Marsala and served alongside the *gnocchi*

➤ I haven't tried it, but I dare say a peach, sliced in eighths and heated in the boozy, buttery syrup, would be very fine here too

ICE CREAM *see also pages 41, 80, 89*

I have spent many a happy hour making ice cream. I was given a little machine some time ago that turns a strawberry purée and some sugar syrup into the most sublime *sorbet de fraise* in half an hour or so, particularly if I slop in a couple of spoonfuls of thick yogurt before it has finished. Before the machine I used to make ice cream in the freezer, taking the mixture out every hour or so to stir it as it froze. That was when I had a freezer. And the time to make it.

On the weekend, from early spring to late autumn, I use my machine, though it is better at sorbet than creamy ice. During the week I am happy to buy my ice cream and always like to have a carton in the freezer compartment at the top of the refrigerator. It's usually vanilla. There is little wrong with bought ice creams—some are really quite good, though I must say I find many too sweet and their texture boringly consistent. What I would really like to get hold of are the ices of my childhood, the ones made by small dairies.

Those ices had character. They were more milky than creamy, and were a treat to be enjoyed on shopping trips, when my parents would take me out for tea in a department store. I can clearly remember the strawberry ices in their little silver dishes with condensation running down the outside. Now that was ice cream—replaced in later years with the brands we know so well, made with vegetable fat instead of dairy products and hardly worthy of the name ice cream.

➤ You can only make good ice cream with good ingredients. Vegetable fat is not one of them. For the best ice cream look out for those that contain cream, sugar, and eggs

A FEW GOOD THINGS TO POUR, SCATTER, OR SPOON OVER ICE CREAM . . .

➤ Maple syrup: make sure that what you are buying is the real thing; avoid bottles with labels that say Maple Flavor Syrup. Particularly suitable for coffee and walnut ices

➤ Chocolate shavings: peel curls or shavings of chocolate from a bittersweet bar with a vegetable peeler. This is easiest when taken from the flat of the bar and when the chocolate is at room temperature. Best for vanilla or coffee ices

➤ Granola: crunchy oats and dried fruit are a surprisingly good topping for vanilla and chocolate ices

➤ Toasted nuts: the secret is to toast the nuts till golden. Let them burn and they will be bitter. A sprinkling of sugar before toasting, particularly over almonds, is unnecessary but satisfyingly crunchy. Sliced almonds are best with strawberry ice cream, walnuts (toasted, then rubbed to remove some of their papery skins) with coffee, and hazelnuts (same treatment, then toasted again) over chocolate

➤ Pistachios: shelled and chopped, no need to toast, scattered over strawberry ice cream

➤ Brittle, *turrón*, and *praline*: glistening shards of nuts in glassy caramel add an exhilarating crunch. Crush with a rolling pin or bang with a hammer. Best of all as partners for berry ice creams and sorbets

➤ M and M's: a sweet, childishly indulgent crunch to scatter over vanilla ice cream

➤ Chocolate sauce: see page 126

➤ Fruits in alcohol: a jar of fruits preserved in alcohol and a carton of ice cream is one of the most delectable desserts I can think of, particularly if the ice cream is vanilla and the fruit is pears in *eau de vie*. Cherries in brandy and prunes in Armagnac are easy to find at gourmet stores and can be stored almost indefinitely. A first-class pantry dessert

AND SORBETS . . .

➤ Generally speaking, sorbets do not respond favorably to embellishment, though a shot of compatible liquor is unlikely to go amiss:

Raspberry—*eau de vie de framboise*
Pear—*eau de vie Poire Williams*
Lemon—vodka
Black currant—*crème de cassis*, an intensely fruity mouthful

Or, of course, a little of the fruit with which the sorbet has been made

Instant Raspberry Ice Cream

FOR 4

1 cup whipping cream   *10 ounces frozen raspberries*

Put the cream and the frozen fruit (it must be frozen) into the food processor or blender. Whizz on low speed till the fruit and cream form a pink creamy mass. You have ice cream.

➤ To save you the trouble of trying it out, this idea doesn't work with frozen black currants and is not much better with strawberries. Stick to raspberries

Instant Raspberry Sorbet

Whizz a package of frozen raspberries to slush in the food processor. Divide it quickly among wineglasses. Upend a measure of *framboise* over the result and call it raspberry sorbet.

Espresso Ice Cream

As I said earlier, I love dishes where hot and cold are played off against one another. Shockingly cold ice cream with hot, slightly bitter coffee is one that I think works especially well. Sweeten the espresso if you wish, but make sure that the two components are very cold and very hot.

FOR 2

4 large balls of vanilla or   *2* demitasses *of hot, strong*
   coffee ice cream   *espresso coffee*

Put the balls of ice cream, in pairs, into large cups or small dishes. Pour the hot coffee over and eat with a teaspoon.

The Ice Cream Sundae

People come over all snooty about ice cream sundaes. And well they might. A mess of canned fruit with vegetable-fat ice cream and chocolate syrup is a travesty. But a true ice cream sundae can be a thing of joy: some puréed and a few whole fresh loganberries or raspberries, vanilla ice cream or chocolate ice cream, and melted bitter chocolate and coffee liqueur. Try vanilla ice cream in a tall glass with sliced fresh peaches and raspberry purée or just a glass of proper strawberry ice cream with fresh strawberries and a sauce made from the fruit sharpened with lemon juice. A good ice cream sundae is a true celebration of fine ice cream and ripe fruit. And what is wrong with that?

A Few Sundae Suggestions

Tall, thick glasses and long-handled spoons are *de rigueur*

➤ Sliced purple figs, small scoops of mascarpone cheese, and larger ones of vanilla ice cream drizzled with raspberry purée

➤ Orange sorbet, the juice and seeds from a passion fruit, and slices of fresh pineapple

➤ Vanilla ice cream, hot chocolate sauce, and slices of ripe, juicy pears

➤ Broken baked meringue, softly whipped cream, vanilla ice cream, and raspberries crushed slightly with a fork. A dollop of raspberry purée (fresh berries whizzed in the blender with a teaspoon of lemon juice) wouldn't go amiss either

➤ Sliced bananas, neither too thin nor too ripe, vanilla ice cream, the juice and seeds of a passion fruit, and a little cream. Go over the top with toasted sliced almonds if you want

➤ Prunes in brandy or Armagnac, *fromage blanc*, and chocolate ice cream. Tip over a measure of the prune liquor as you eat

A Few Quick Sauces for Ice Cream, Poached Fruits, and Their Like

Quick Black-Currant Sauce
Frozen black currants make a wonderful sauce in more or less 10 minutes. Tip an 8-ounce package of frozen black currants into a stainless-steel pan, add a tablespoon or two of water, and cover. Cook over gentle heat for 5-6 minutes, till they start to burst, then add sugar to taste. Spoon hot over cold ice cream or poached pears or stir into thick, plain yogurt. You can do the same thing with blueberries.

Shiny Chocolate Sauce

6 ounces finest semisweet or
bittersweet chocolate
4 tablespoons butter
¼ cup sugar

2 tablespoons golden syrup or
light corn syrup
1 cup milk

Break the chocolate into pieces and melt it, with the butter, in a bowl over a pan of hot water. Stir in the sugar and syrup until dissolved, then pour in the milk and continue to cook for 10 minutes, until the sauce thickens.

Vanilla Fudge Sauce

A thick fudge sauce that for once tastes more of vanilla than sugar. The vanilla is the secret: use the finest quality vanilla extract that I go on about in the introduction, rather than vanilla flavoring.

4 tablespoons butter
½ packed cup brown sugar
⅓ cup golden syrup or
light corn syrup

vanilla extract
⅔ cup whipping cream

Put everything except the vanilla extract and cream into a heavy-based saucepan. Leave over a medium heat till all has dissolved, then turn the heat up slightly and let the mixture bubble away gently for 5 minutes. No longer. Add a few drops of vanilla extract—depending on the quality you have you may need anything up to a teaspoon—then pour in the cream. Give the mixture a good stir, and set aside to cool. It will thicken more quickly if you pour the sauce into a cool, but heatproof, pitcher. Use in sundaes, or over baked bananas.

CHOCOLATE *see also pages 53, 126*

Chocolate, like olive oil, is something that is taken more seriously nowadays. Some people, I venture, might even brag about bars of expensive and difficult-to-obtain chocolate just as others do bottles of "estate-bottled, cold-pressed, extra-virgin olive oil." Another culinary status symbol.

When I refer to chocolate in the recipes and ideas that follow I mean fine chocolate, not candy. The difference is easy to spot even before you taste it. Take two bars of chocolate, one a well-known brand name that we have known since childhood and the other a fine, more expensive bar such as, say, Valrhona or Barry. The former will break softly while the latter will snap crisply; the texture of the cheaper chocolate will be fudgy, grainy, and soft. Its color will be a pale dull brown. The fine bar will be shiny and smooth, a lovely dark, rich, browny-black.

Taste them. The fine stuff tastes instantly of chocolate, not sugar. But there is no real bitterness there either. There may be a faint fruitiness about it or a tinge of coffee. You will probably be left with the flavor of chocolate, but your mouth will feel clean. Now taste the chocolate bar, which I prefer to call candy. It instantly coats the roof of the mouth. It feels greasy and cloying on the palate. That is because it contains vegetable fat or oil and sugar.

For desserts that taste of chocolate rather than sugar and grease you should look for chocolate that contains over 47 percent cocoa solids. I have met some with as little as 17 percent and as high as 90 percent. I part company with many other writers and cooks over Swiss chocolate, which I find too creamy, sweet and inferior to the French brands. Green and Black's, an organic chocolate, is a favorite of mine, with a deep chocolate flavor and a slight bitterness that I enjoy. Those interested in such things might note that fine chocolate contains considerably fewer calories than the candy-bar type.

Beware that what you are buying is not something called "artificial chocolate" or "confectionary coating." In my book these are two of the nastiest food products ever created and the most that can be said of them is that they are brown and sweet. Fine chocolate is available from gourmet grocers and many supermarkets. It may at first seem expensive, but it goes further as it has more flavor and the dessert you end up with will have an infinitely better taste. Like most good things, the finest chocolate can seem addictive (though some so-called "chocoholics" may find they are actually addicted to sugar) and once hooked there is no going back to the cheap stuff.

Chocolate for Dessert

A bar of fine chocolate is a good friend to the fast foodie. Chocolate desserts can be as simple as dipping a thin, nutty cookie into a pot of melted chocolate, or as sophisticated as a hot chocolate soufflé. One of the most successful fast desserts I regularly offer, though something of a cheat, is a plate of different chocolate pieces. The better quality chocolates have surprisingly individual characters, and snapped into jagged shards rather than cut in neat triangles, a mixed plate always seems to go down well.

Melting Chocolate

If you want smooth, voluptuous melted chocolate, and I assume you do, it is worth taking a little care. All will end in tears if you melt your expensive chocolate over too high a heat, or stir it too much.

Break the chocolate, which will snap keenly if it is good stuff, into pieces 1 inch or so square. Ignore anyone who says you need to chop it finely. Put the pieces in a heat-proof china or glass bowl and set over a pan of water. The pan should be of a size that the bowl sits comfortably in the top. Put the pan over high heat, turning the heat down as soon as the water comes to a boil (and not a minute later). The water should do little more than shudder.

Leave the chocolate alone. Do not stir it. It is ready when there are no lumps of solid chocolate left (this is not as obvious as it seems because they tend to lurk under the surface). Remove from the heat and gently stir the liquid chocolate. It will remain shiny, smooth, and liquid until the water cools.

A Few Good Things to do with Melted Chocolate

➤ Give each diner a tiny coffee cup full of warm chocolate and a handful of things to dip in it:
amaretti cookies
ladyfingers
those Italian cigarette wafer cookies
slices of underripe pear
pieces of toasted brioche

➤ Drizzle over peeled and thinly sliced oranges or bananas

➤ Pour over halved, cored, and poached pears

A quick dessert that always seems to go down well is something dipped in chocolate. It takes barely 20 minutes to dry in a cool room and can continue drying while you eat the rest of your meal.

Chocolate-Dipped *Praline*

I often serve lumps of *praline* or nut brittle dipped in chocolate instead of a dessert. Best to snap the nutty caramel into mouth-sized pieces before dipping, as they are awkward to break later. Dip each piece halfway into a pot of melted chocolate and leave on wax paper to dry. Pile on a small plate and pass around with the coffee.

Chocolate Almonds

Take a couple of handfuls of shelled but not skinned almonds. Place in a dry frying pan and cook till fragrant, or broil them if it is easier. Let them cool. Melt 4 ounces of fine chocolate over hot water as on page 128. Toss the almonds into the chocolate and stir till they are covered.

Dust a piece of wax paper generously with unsweetened cocoa powder—it really must be the finest stuff—then lift each almond out of the chocolate with a small spoon and drop onto the cocoa-covered paper. Roll them gently in the cocoa and leave to cool. You will probably wish you had made more.

Ricotta with Chocolate and Cognac

The cocoa powder you use is all-important. That designed for instant hot drinks is not the same: it contains sugar and is pretty nasty anyway. Make sure that the cocoa is better than the average; the Dutch or French brands have a superior flavor.

FOR 2

¼ cup raisins	2 heaped tablespoons sugar
1 tablespoon cognac	2 heaped tablespoons
½ cup ricotta cheese	unsweetened cocoa powder
⅓ cup fromage blanc	brandy snaps or other cookies,
or petit suisse	to serve

Put the raisins in a cup. Pour the cognac over and leave for 10 minutes. Push the ricotta through a sieve into a bowl and stir in the *fromage blanc* or *petit suisse*. Stir in the sugar and cocoa powder, then the soaked raisins and any liquid they have failed to absorb.

Chill for 15 minutes, or longer if you have it. (Any longer than that and you should cover it to stop it getting "fridgey.") Serve in small pots or cups, with brandy snaps or other crisp cookies.

Bread and Chocolate: A Midmorning Pick-me-up

It seems the oddest of all combinations, bread and chocolate. But a light airy bun, one of the flat ones with a little flour on top, is quite delightful as a snack when split and eaten with squares of fine chocolate. I didn't believe it either till I tried it. If the fickleness of fashion has had your baker swapping his floury buns for holey Italian ciabatta, don't worry—it will work just as well.

➤ Chocolate does nothing for peaches, strawberries, or kiwi fruit

CHOCOLATE TRUFFLE CAKE

Chocolate truffle cakes have two extremes: the ubiquitous mousse-like cake on every restaurant menu, from steak houses to three-star temples of gastronomy, and the slabs from supermarket bakeries. I don't rate either of them particularly highly. Most bakery cakes taste stale even when they are not, and most restaurant cakes tend to leave me dead from the waist up.

The dessert that follows offers something of the professionalism and decadence of the former with the homey, crumb crust of the latter. When I want a slice of hopelessly rich chocolate cake, and I lack the time to make Alice Waters's ultimate version from her book *Chez Panisse Desserts*, then the following recipe is the one I currently use. It was given to me by Christabel Gairdner, as if she hasn't contributed enough to this book already, and is a favorite of friends of hers.

I particularly like the idea that just over a pint of cream, a pound of chocolate, and a package of graham crackers will give me a dessert, even though it is the very devil to cut.

It will take you half an hour to make but you will need to allow for setting time.

FOR 8-10

2¼ cups graham cracker crumbs
½ cup butter
1 pound finest quality chocolate

2½ cups whipping cream
unsweetened cocoa powder

Lightly butter a cake pan, about 9 inches in diameter, depending on whether you want a thick or thin cake. I prefer to use a larger diameter pan to produce a slim version. A loose-bottomed pan is pretty much essential; one of those with a springclip will make life even easier.

When crushing the graham crackers, they should be in coarse rather than fine crumbs. Melt the butter in a small pan over medium heat. Stir in the crumbs and mix. Tip the buttered crumbs into the cake pan and press down quite firmly to give a flat crumb base. Refrigerate.

Melt the chocolate as described earlier (in small pieces in a bowl over a pan of simmering water, if you cannot be bothered to check back). Whip the cream to stand in firm peaks, then stir in the melted chocolate, gently but thoroughly. Spoon the chocolate cream over the crumb base and leave in the refrigerator till set. I have known the cake to be ready in a couple of hours, though some like to leave it overnight. Sprinkle with cocoa before serving in small pieces.

CHOCOLATE GINGER

A dark chocolate flatters shining globes of ginger in syrup like nothing else. Mascarpone is something of a foil.

FOR EACH PERSON

a large scoop of mascarpone cheese
3 pieces of preserved stem ginger
in syrup, with a little of the syrup

2 tablespoons melted fine
chocolate

Place a generous scoop of mascarpone in the middle of a small plate. Slice the ginger and scatter loosely around the mascarpone. Drizzle the melted chocolate over the whole plate and eat with a teaspoon. Coffee, strong and hot, will be welcome at this point.

QUICK CHOCOLATE CAKE

Fifteen minutes to make and fifteen to bake is about as fast as a decent chocolate cake gets. I should, of course, mention it needs a good hour to cool though. As always, the finer the chocolate, the finer the result.

I am very partial to a thin slice of rich chocolate cake— a small slice, without any ghastly butter cream or chocolate frosting, that is. To my mind it is only really good when spongy at the edge and fudgy in the middle. The following recipe is just that: a shallow cake with a center similar to chocolate mousse, the whole thing given bite with chopped toasted hazelnuts. More of a dessert than a teatime cake, I am not sure it needs any embellishment, except, perhaps, a dollop of sharp *crème fraîche* if you must.

FOR 10

5 ounces fine chocolate	½ cup + 1 tablespoon all-
⅔ cup shelled hazelnuts	purpose flour
2 tablespoons butter	¼ cup unsweetened cocoa
2 tablespoons whipping cream	powder, plus a little for
5 eggs, separated	dusting the finished cake
3 heaped tablespoons sugar	

You will need a springform cake pan about 8 inches in diameter, buttered and dusted with a little flour.

Set the oven to 350°F. Break the chocolate into pieces and put it in a small bowl set over a pan of simmering water. See the melting chocolate instructions on page 128. Put the hazelnuts on a baking sheet and toast them in the oven till the skins crack and flake. Rub them with a dish towel; most of the skins will flake off. Chop them roughly, either with a large knife or in a food processor. Return them to the oven until they are golden brown.

When the chocolate has melted, stir in the butter, in little chunks, and the cream. Remove from the heat. Beat the egg whites till they stand in peaks; this will take seconds with an electric mixer. Fold in the sugar with a metal spoon. Do this tenderly but thoroughly.

Stir the egg yolks quickly into the chocolate, butter, and cream. Fold in the flour, cocoa, and hazelnuts. Fold this in turn into the egg-whites and sugar. You must be careful here; the point is to mix the chocolate and the egg white mixtures scrupulously so that there are no streaks of white yet the mixture is still light and full of air. Be thorough and gentle; a large metal spoon will be a help. The result will be rather like an unset chocolate mousse.

Pour it into the pan, scraping every little bit out of the bowl with a rubber spatula. Bake in the preheated oven for 15 minutes. The outer edges of the cake will be firm, like a sponge cake, the middle rather wobbly. If you take it out now the cake will have a creamy soft center. If you prefer something more cake-like, then leave it in for a further 5 or 7 minutes. Any longer and you might as well have made an ordinary chocolate sponge cake.

Remove and cool. After 10 minutes or so, slide a metal spatula around the edge and remove the side of the pan. Leave the cake on its base to cool. Dust with cocoa powder if you wish, but it is not essential. Serve in small slices, on large plates, perhaps with *crème fraîche*.

Hot Chocolate Soufflé

This is so easy. Everyone will be suitably impressed and think you are a genius. Which, of course, you are.

FOR 2 LARGE, INDIVIDUAL SOUFFLÉS

4 ounces fine chocolate
a little butter
¼ cup sugar

3 large eggs, separated
confectioners' sugar, for dusting

Set the oven to 400°F. Break the chocolate into bits and melt in a bowl over hot water. Follow the melting chocolate instructions on page 128.

While the oven is heating and the chocolate is melting, rub a little butter around the inside of each of two soufflé dishes. They should be the large individual size, the ones that hold 1½ cups. Or you could make four smaller soufflés if your dishes are tiny. Sprinkle a little of the sugar around the buttered dishes, then shake the excess back into the rest of the sugar.

Whisk the egg yolks and sugar till creamy; the mixture doesn't have to be thick. A matter of seconds with an electric mixer. Wash the beaters and dry carefully, then beat the egg whites till they stand in stiff peaks. Remove the chocolate mixture from the heat and stir it into the egg yolks and sugar. Do this thoroughly but gently.

Working quickly, scoop half of the egg whites into the chocolate, mix gently but thoroughly, and then scrape the mixture back into the egg whites. Mix carefully. A metal spoon, as large as you have, is best for this. What you want to end up with is a rich, chocolatey mixture without lumps of egg white, but mixed tenderly enough that it is still light and full of air.

Using a rubber spatula, scrape the mixture into the soufflé dishes. They should be full to within ½ inch or so of the top. Bake in the preheated oven for 15 minutes. They are done when they are risen, slightly spongy around the edges, and creamy in the middle. Dust with confectioners' sugar if you feel like it.

➤ You can look inside the oven to see if they are ready without disaster, but don't slam the oven door afterward

➤ Your friends must wait for their soufflé, not the other way around: it will hold up for a minute or two, but not much more. Don't push your luck. They should be seated and ready to eat as the soufflé comes from the oven. This is really the best dessert to serve to a special friend at an informal meal in the kitchen. If you insist on doing eight of them for a dinner party you are either a masochist or trying to prove something. Don't blame me if it all ends in tears

➤ The inside should be really quite creamy. Cook the soufflés a little too long and you will have a more solid texture, rather like a cake. In this case, serve them from their dish, with cream, and call them chocolate puddings

➤ Don't worry if your souffles don't rise perfectly all the way around like some whiz-kid chef's. Yours may rise more on one side than the other. They may even crack a little on top. Yours will be better than the chef's perfect version. Yours will have charm. And, anyway, no one likes a smart aleck

LEMONS

I feel lost without a lemon in the kitchen. From a dessert point of view, lemons are nigh on essential for adding acidity to balance the oversweet and for bringing out the flavor of some fruits and preventing the discoloration of others. They are equally useful as a major ingredient in their own right.

Use them as principal flavorings for desserts where a balance of richness and piquancy is needed: a fresh-tasting syllabub, the sugar and cream given tang by lemon juice; an absurdly rich pot of *crème fraîche* and yogurt stirred through with lemon curd and served in miniature pots; or just lemon juice as the major flavoring for crêpes hot from the pan.

Choosing Lemons
The only way to tell if a lemon is worth the money is to squeeze it. You will have to ignore the looks of disapproval from the greengrocer. A good lemon is a ripe one, and there are fewer about than you might imagine. They should be firm but not rock hard, and heavy for their size. The real hard whoppers invariably yield little juice. Those slightly softer, medium-sized

and thin-skinned, seem to be more generously endowed with juice, though less easy to grate.

Much of the joy of a lemon is in its zest, the aromatic yellow skin where most of the flavor is contained. Zest is a very appropriate word. Unfortunately, the average lemon has been plied with fungicides, pesticides, and waxes to make it more appealing to the eye, which means that grating an unwashed lemon into your cake mix is tantamount to adding a teaspoon of chemicals too.

Lemons straight from the tree do not shine dazzlingly. They have a gentle hue to them. You can find untreated lemons in some major stores and, of course, healthfood and wholefood markets. But they are far from accessible to most of us, so my advice is to wash your lemons under running water, though avoid scrubbing them so hard you take off the top layer of zest.

Grating Lemons
Overzealous grating will lead to bitterness. What you want is the thin yellow top coat of the skin: it's where the best of the lemon's flavor lurks. The white layer beneath is mouth-puckeringly bitter. It's called the pith, and should be left on the fruit rather than stirred into the dessert. So go easy with the grater, and use the small holes.

LEMON SYLLABUB

All recipes for lemon syllabub include a statutory overnight marinating of lemon zest in brandy. This act, though simplicity in itself, may well be the reason for this delightful dessert's fall from grace. The quick, perhaps heretical, method below includes grating the lemon zest instead—just the way they do in most restaurants.

FOR 4, WITH SECOND HELPINGS

1 lemon
2 tablespoons brandy
6 tablespoons sweet sherry

6 tablespoons sugar
1¼ cups whipping cream

Grate the zest from the lemon on the fine side of the grater, taking care not to include the bitter white pith underneath. Put to one side. Cut the lemon in half and squeeze the juice into a large mixing bowl. Add the brandy and sherry. Stir in the sugar till pretty well dissolved.

Add the cream in a steady stream, electric beaters in one hand, cream in the other Take care that you are not beating too fast, in which case it will become buttery and grainy very suddenly. A balloon whisk will give better control if you can bear it. When the cream leaves a soft trail from the beaters, and settles in drifts rather than peaks, it is ready. Stir in the grated zest. Spoon into glasses and chill for a few minutes.

LITTLE POTS OF LEMON CREAM

If richness alone could be a measure of excellence then these pots of lemon cream would win hands down. To all but the most serious lemon-dessert addicts their tart unctuousness may overwhelm.

FOR 2

4 heaped tablespoons good lemon curd
2 heaped tablespoons thick plain yogurt
2 heaped tablespoons crème fraîche
1 heaped teaspoon finely grated lemon zest

Stir together the ingredients, then spoon into tiny glasses, *demitasse* coffee cups, or even egg cups. Dot with a crystallized violet—a proper one, not one of those purple sugar impostors. Chill for 10 minutes, and eat with a teaspoon.

Cheeses for Spring

I quite often break off a lump of cheese, or slice it if that is more appropriate, to eat at the end of my meal. I have lost interest, and I never had very much, in the cellophane-wrapped specimens at the chill counter. They all taste like soap to me. Even the well-aged ones are just sharp; they have no real depth of flavor. You can't beat a piece cut from a farmhouse or artisan cheese, properly made in the traditional manner, and preferably with unpasteurized milk. Fortunately, one can buy fine cheese in some supermarkets as well as in specialist cheese shops.

Among other firm British cheeses good to eat in March, April, and May is Cheshire; choose an orange-fleshed, unpasteurized one. Many of the Cheddars widely available in the U. S. will make very fine eating now. A cheese specialist will guide you to a Cheddar that is right, but you can really only tell if it is the one for you by tasting it. If you go to a cheese shop they will probably have several Cheddars to choose from.

SUMMER

Fast food is somehow especially pertinent to summer. I will go to extreme lengths not to put the oven on on a warm summer evening. If I can be persuaded to cook at all it will be something of the minimum fuss, maximum effect variety. Desserts, too, at this time of year must involve as little preparation and cooking as possible. At the very height of the season, with temperatures as high as they go, all I am really interested in is twenty new ways to serve a ripe melon.

An abundance of fine-flavored fruit means that desserts can be prepared in minutes all summer long. The simpler the idea, the more pleasing the result—a glass of red berries topped up with Sauternes, a bowl of strawberries showered with mellow balsamic vinegar, or cubes of refreshing melon scattered with shredded basil leaves.

After a generous plate of leafy salad, or perhaps some cold pasta dressed with olive oil and fresh young garlic, I want nothing more than a dish of perfectly ripe fruit. If something a little more substantial is required I may mix it with some cheese—watermelon and feta perhaps, or, a great favorite of mine, goat cheese and cherries. Whether your interests lie in a bowl of raspberries, warm from the sun, or a compote of raspberries and blueberries as rich as red velvet, fruit is the backbone of summer desserts.

CHERRIES

I said in *Real Fast Food* that cherries only inspire me when they are eaten from the stem out of the greengrocer's brown paper bag. If I am to eat them at all they must have a little tartness to them, and be deep red or yellow and vermilion in color. Sweet, black varieties leave me cold.

Cherries and *Chèvre*

The second best way with cherries is to eat them with goat cheese. Choose a soft, fresh *chèvre*. An ash-covered log is ideal. Slice it in rounds, about ½ inch thick, and lay two or three on each plate. Drop a handful of ripe red and yellow cherries, stems attached, over each one. Unless the *chèvre* is very soft I usually push a little of the cheese onto each cherry with my knife as I eat.

HOT CHERRIES WITH CALVADOS

One of the few hot summer desserts that are worth the trouble. Expect it to take a full ten minutes of your time.

FOR 4

1 pound cherries　　　　　　　*vanilla ice cream,* fromage
2 tablespoons butter　　　　　　blanc, *or thick plain*
¼ cup sugar　　　　　　　　　*yogurt, to serve*
2 tablespoons Calvados
　or cognac

Pull the stems from the cherries. Melt the butter in a frying pan, add the sugar and the Calvados or cognac, and mix well over the heat. Throw in the cherries and toss them around gently in the bubbling mixture. Cook over high heat till they start to caramelize. Lift the cherries from the pan with a slotted spoon and divide among four warm plates. Add a dollop of ice cream, *fromage blanc,* or thick yogurt at the side.

STRAWBERRIES *see also pages 76, 98, 167, 171, 177*

A bowl of ripe strawberries and cream is one of the fastest desserts there is. And yet it can be bettered so easily, particularly if you keep the cream for raspberries, and sprinkle the straw-berries with a little sugar and red wine instead. If cream it must be, then at least invest in some *crème fraîche*, whose slight sharp-ness will lift the flavor of the fruit, and whose unctuousness will contrast with the fruit's crunchy seeds.

There are probably over a hundred varieties of strawberry. Stafford Whiteaker's fascinating little book on strawberries mentions one and a half dozen, Edward Bunyard's *Anatomy of Dessert* a good two dozen. Ken Muir, the British strawberry specialist, stocks even more than that. But these are gardeners' strawberries, though there is no reason why a few plants cannot survive on a warm windowsill. Then you wouldn't even have to shop for them.

In the markets, however, we are hardly ever given a choice, even though many of their seasons overlap. Here, at the moment, we know only if they are French, English, or Californian, and this fact tells us little about the flavor.

Choosing strawberries is fraught with difficulties. Here are a few points that might help you to avoid disappointment.

➤ Check the bottom of the basket to make sure it is dry. If it is stained with juice the berries at the bottom will be past it

➤ Buy your berries from a greengrocer you know, someone who is not likely to sell you baskets containing squashy fruit under a few good-looking berries

➤ Supermarket strawberries often have a hole in the top of the packaging; sniff the berries through it—if they are fragrant then they may well be good to eat

➤ A little whiteness around the top is not always a bad sign. Such berries will respond to a short time in a warm room, or can be perked up with balsamic vinegar (see page 145)

➤ I am sorry, but hugeness of size is not a guarantee of flavor. Plump and red to look at, the berries may be utterly tasteless to eat

➤ I find the best way to perk up slightly underripe strawberries or those short on flavor is to slice them in half and place them in a bowl with a sprinkling of sugar. Set aside in a covered bowl for half an hour before eating

STRAWBERRIES AND CREAM

I was brought up on strawberries and evaporated milk, the thought of which now makes me shudder. The boiled taste of the thin cream is not that far removed from that of ultra-pasteurized cream, which has been heated to such a temperature that its flavor has gone too. Look out instead for cream from small dairies. You must expect to pay more for it. But it is worth it.

In Britian, yellow cream from Jersey cows is the best, though not as suitable as the piquant French-style *crème fraîche*. The latter is much easier to find nowadays; even my small grocer's shop stocks it. Much other cream is pale and thin. And taste-less. If it was unpasteurized I am sure its flavor would be even better. But bureaucrats who have no tastebuds and hysterical do-gooders have put paid to such treats.

STRAWBERRIES IN BEAUJOLAIS

Slice washed strawberries into a china bowl. Sprinkle with beaujolais, or some other light, fruity red wine. Set aside in a cool place for as long as you can. Half an hour should just about do it.

STRAWBERRIES WITH BLACK PEPPER

The instruction "strawberries taste good with a grinding of black pepper" is hardly news, but a little more detail is needed if the dish is to be a success.

The pepper must, absolutely must, be from freshly ground black peppercorns. It should be finely ground but far from dust, and it should be done very, very sparingly.

The point is to heighten the natural flavor of the berry with-out noticeably adding any pepperiness.

Strawberries with Basil

If I want a little pepperiness with my strawberries I would rather add basil, the herb whose aromatic leaves have a similar but more subtle effect.

FOR 2

½ pound strawberries
a little lemon juice

1 heaped tablespoon finely shredded basil leaves

Remove the hulls from the strawberries and cut each fruit in half. Sprinkle with lemon juice, then scatter the shredded basil leaves over. Toss the fruit very gently with a large spoon. Leave for 15 or 20 minutes at room temperature before eating.

Strawberries with Passion Fruit

Cut a heavy, wrinkled passion fruit in half. Squeeze its orange juice and little black seeds with their golden halo over a bowl of hulled and halved strawberries. Cover with a plate and leave for 15 minutes. Lift the lid, inhale the wonderful fragrance, and eat, crunching the little seeds with the soft fruit.

Strawberries with Mint and Orange

Mint has a very pronounced, clean flavor. You won't need much of it to perk up your bowl of berries. Squeeze a generous amount of orange juice over a bowl of hulled berries. You will need the juice of 2 large oranges to each pound of strawberries. Snip some tiny, sweet mint leaves into little bits, then stir them gently into the fruit and juice. Two or three sprigs of the herb is all you will need for a pound or so of the berries.

AND WITH CASSIS

Crème de cassis, the intensely fruity black-currant liqueur, flatters rather than bullies a bowl of berries.

1 pound strawberries, hulled
2 tablespoons crème de cassis

thick plain yogurt,
to serve

Cut the berries in half, sprinkle them with the *cassis*, and set aside at room temperature for 15 minutes. Eat with spoonfuls of thick yogurt.

AND WITH BALSAMIC VINEGAR

Marcella Hazan, the doyenne of Italian food writers whose thoroughly researched and tested recipes put most others to shame, is probably responsible for bringing this bizarre-sounding idea to our attention. It has a heavenly fragrance, deeply sweet and rich, and is my favorite way of all to eat strawberries.

The point she makes in her book, *Marcella's Kitchen*, is that the vinegar is especially good for perking up strawberries that are not yet ripe. "As though they had been penetrated by the most ardent of summer suns," is how she describes the result of macerating unripe berries in the mellow brown liquid.

Remove the leaves and hulls, cut large berries in half, and put them in a bowl. Add a little sugar, perhaps 2 heaped tablespoons per pound of fruit. Set aside for 25 minutes or so (an hour would be better), until the strawberries have released some of their juices to form a light syrup with the sugar. Add the balsamic vinegar—1 tablespoon to the pound.

AND WITH LIME JUICE

Much better than lemon or orange I think. Cut a lime in half and squeeze its juice over the fruit. Eat immediately.

Strawberries with Rose-Petal Cream

A straightforward enough recipe from Joyce Molyneux's restaurant, The Carved Angel in Dartmouth in Devon, England. The soft rose fragrance is delightful with the ripe fruit. Claret-colored, deeply perfumed, old-fashioned roses are the ones for this. Make sure you know that they haven't been sprayed with pesticide. You can either layer the cream and fruit in glasses as they do at the restaurant, or serve it on a plate, surrounding a pile of ripe berries. Either way, this fragrant dessert couldn't be easier.

FOR 4-6

1 fragrant, dark red rose   *lemon juice*
1¼ cups whipping cream   *1 pound strawberries*
1 heaped tablespoon sugar

Separate the rose petals. Whizz them with half of the cream, the sugar, and a dash of lemon juice in a blender. Mix with the remaining cream and whip lightly. Hull the strawberries and halve if large. Layer with the rose-petal cream in a single bowl or in individual glasses.

Strawberry Fool

Lumpy with chunks of fruit and sharpened by *fromage blanc*, this is a fool far better than the toothpaste-like commercial ones.

FOR 2

½ pound strawberries, hulled   *½ cup* crème fraîche
1 cup fromage blanc   *or thick whipping cream*

Crush the berries in a bowl with a fork. Fold in the *fromage blanc* and the *crème fraîche* or cream, slowly but thoroughly. Spoon into glasses or small pots and chill before serving—leave it for as long as possible. An almond cookie or shortbread would make a flattering accompaniment.

Strawberries with Syllabub Sauce

FOR 4

½ cup sugar
1¼ cups whipping cream
¼ cup Marsala or
 medium dry sherry
1 teaspoon vanilla extract
 (not flavoring)

finely grated zest and juice of
 1 orange
1 pound strawberries

Put the sugar, cream, Marsala or sherry, vanilla, and orange zest and juice in a mixing bowl. Beat with an electric mixer till thick and creamy, but not actually stiff. Remove the hulls from the strawberries; cut the fruit in quarters. Put them in the bottom of four large balloon wineglasses or small china bowls.

Spoon the syllabub mixture over the strawberries. Refrigerate till needed, but for at least 20 minutes if you can.

Raspberries *see also pages 55, 124, 164, 165, 171, 175*

Lightly crushed against the side of the bowl, raspberries reveal a fragrance that, combined with a little warmth from the sun, is positively intoxicating.

The deeper red the fruit, the more luscious it will be to eat. Pale pink raspberries hold few pleasures. Choose unblemished, dark-colored fruits. Check them for flavor by carefully sniffing them; if their fragrance is obvious they will probably be good. Some of the French raspberries appearing early in the season smell almost alcoholic, as if someone has spilled *framboise* over them.

Much as I love raspberries I will not confine them to being eaten with nothing but cream, perfection though such simplicity can be. Raspberries and their sister berries have enough clout that they can be used in pastries, fruit salads, compotes, and trifles. Raspberries, unlike strawberries, were made for cream. They make the finest of syllabubs and finish a close second to gooseberries in the fools' race.

Berries on a Leaf

An absurdly easy and beautiful presentation. It will impress even those used to the most elaborate of desserts.

Cover a plain white plate with raspberry or rose leaves, then carefully pile, a handful at a time, the velvet berries as high as you can. Serve a pitcher of cream and a bowl of sugar on the side.

Raspberries in Gewürztraminer

Drop a handful of the berries into a glass of chilled sweetish wine. Gewürztraminer would suit, though others spring to mind like Muscatel or Beaumes de Venise.

Raspberries with Pistachios

Tip the berries into a bowl. Shell the pistachios (you will need a small handful of shelled nuts for each basket of berries), then chop them coarsely with a knife. Scatter them over the fruit.

Raspberries with Almonds

FOR 4

½ pound raspberries (2 cups) *1 cup cake crumbs*
¼ cup sugar *½ cup whipping cream*
⅓ cup minced almonds

Put the berries into a small saucepan with the sugar and cook till the juices leak from the fruit and the sugar has dissolved, about 3 minutes over medium heat.

Fold the almonds and the cake crumbs into the fruit and its juice, then spoon into small glasses. Chill in the refrigerator, then pour the cream over the top. Eat at once.

Raspberries and Cream

The finest of all marriages, dark, blood-red raspberries and rich yellow cream. Offer *crème fraîche* for its piquancy, and a bowl of sugar for its pleasant crystalline grittiness as much as its sweetness.

RASPBERRY FOOL

FOR 4

½ pound raspberries (2 cups)   1 cup whipping cream
1 teaspoon lemon juice   softly whipped

Whizz the raspberries in the food processor till smooth. Add the lemon juice, then fold in the softly whipped cream. Serve in glasses with crisp cookies.

ANOTHER RASPBERRY FOOL

FOR 4

½ pound raspberries (2 cups)   ½ cup thick plain yogurt
⅔ cup whipping cream

Whizz half the berries till smooth. Whip the cream until it forms soft peaks, and stir in the yogurt and then the puréed berries. Fold in the reserved whole berries and spoon into four glasses.

ICED RASPBERRY FOOL

Whizz, stir, whip, fold, freeze.

FOR 4

1 pound raspberries (4 cups)   1 cup whipping cream
¼ cup sugar

Whizz the raspberries in a food processor.
Stir in the sugar.
Whip the cream till it forms soft peaks.
Gently fold the fruit purée into the cream.
Tip into a bowl and freeze for 2 hours.

Raspberry Syllabub

Making this syllabub was a daily task during the summer and autumn when I once worked in the kitchens of a castle turned restaurant. It was an afternoon job, done when all was peaceful. Sometimes we would run out and I would have to whip one up quickly in the middle of a very busy service. It has remained one of my favorite real fast desserts ever since.

FOR 4

½ pound raspberries (2 cups)
⅓ cup sugar
1 tablespoon framboise *or*
  rosewater

1 cup whipping cream
⅔ cup sweet white wine

Put half of the raspberries into a large bowl and crush them gently against the side with a metal spoon. They will bleed a little. Sprinkle with the sugar and the *framboise* or rosewater. Whip the cream with an electric mixer or whisk until it starts to thicken. It should be thick and unctuous and will slowly fall from the spoon. It must not be what you might call "whipped." Slowly beat the wine into the cream, which must stand in drifts rather than peaks.

Carefully add the cream to the macerating fruit, folding them slowly together with a metal spoon. Throw in the remaining raspberries. Serve in glasses, perhaps with little almond cookies, like the ones the German cookie manufacturers are so good at.

Little Raspberry Soufflés

FOR 4

a little butter and sugar
¾ pound raspberries (3 cups)
6 tablespoons sugar
1 teaspoon framboise, *Kirsch,*
  or neither

3 egg whites
confectioners' sugar, to dust

Rub a little butter around the inside of four small ovenproof molds. They can be those white china ramekins if you have them, or even cups, though not thin porcelain ones. Sprinkle a little sugar over the butter, then turn the dishes upside down and shake out the surplus.

Whizz the raspberries in the processor to form a purée. Add half of the sugar. You can strain the mixture at this point if you hate raspberry seeds. I rather like the mild crunchiness of the little things amid the general smoothness. Add the *framboise* or Kirsch.

Beat the egg whites till stiff; they should stand in peaks. Add the remaining sugar with a metal spoon using a gentle folding motion. Stir a little of the fruit purée into the egg whites and mix gently, then fold the egg whites into the fruit purée. Do this with a large metal spoon as before, gently bringing the mixture up from the bottom and over the egg whites till they are all mixed.

Fill the little dishes or cups with the raspberry mixture. Bake in a preheated 350°F oven until puffed and slightly cracked, about 12 minutes. Dust with a little confectioners' sugar if you wish. Serve immediately.

Almond-Raspberry Pastry

The method looks long here, but it is unlikely to take you more than half an hour or so. It takes five minutes to make the pastry and ten to rest it, fifteen or so to cook it, and ten to cool and decorate it. Hardly an evening's work.

FOR 4

¾ cup all-purpose flour	¼ cup sugar
2 heaped tablespoons ground almonds	1 egg, separated
	extra sugar
pinch of salt	raspberries
6 tablespoons butter	whipping cream

Put the flour and almonds in the food processor with the salt. Add the butter cut in little chunks and whizz for a few seconds till you have what looks like crumbs.

Add the sugar. Whizz once. Add the yolk of the egg and whizz slowly till the whole lot comes together in a big lump. Stop. Turn the dough onto a baking sheet. You won't need to butter it if it's an old one. Press the dough out into a disk about 7 inches in diameter. You can crimp the edges prettily if you wish. I tend not to.

Prick with a fork and rest the pastry in the refrigerator for 10 minutes. (You will probably have to take a lot out to get the sheet in.) Preheat the oven to 400°F. Bake the almond pastry till very pale gold in color, no darker than a piece of shortbread, about 15 minutes. Beat the egg white briefly with a fork and brush a little of it over the pastry. Sprinkle it with a bit of sugar. Return it to the oven to bake for 3 or 4 minutes.

Remove from the oven. Lift the disk carefully onto a cooling rack with the aid of a long, thin spatula. A pancake turner will do. While it is cooling whip the cream into soft peaks.

To assemble, put the almond pastry onto a large plate. Pile the cream in soft waves over the top. Don't fuss about this too much. Place the raspberries on top and eat immediately.

WARMED RASPBERRIES

Tip the raspberries into an ovenproof dish. Sprinkle a little sugar over and leave them in a very low oven, 300°F, for 25 minutes or so. They will have produced copious red juice. Add just a touch, and I mean just a touch, of *crème de cassis* or Kirsch, or, of course, *framboise*. The rich wine-red juices, now heady with raspberries and liqueur, are the point of the thing. Serve in pretty glasses, still warm, with elegant cookies.

OTHER BERRIES AND CURRANTS

I often use a mixture of berries and currants in summer desserts (though I happily use frozen ones in the winter). By a mixture, I mean two or three from a list of purple, black, red, and blue berries: raspberries; tayberries; loganberries and mulberries; red, white, and black currants; blueberries and blackberries. I rarely include strawberries because they become so nasty with the application of heat. I am not sure that there is a right combination of subtle and strident fruits, and often just throw in whatever is on hand. Watch the black currants, though, as they can be overpowering in quantity, especially when up against some of the more unusual red berries.

A PLATE OF CLARET, PURPLE, AND BLUE BERRIES

Tip dusty-blue blueberries, black and dark red blackberries, and glistening loganberries and red currants from their baskets onto a platter. Eaten by candlelight, the berries will sparkle and intrigue, like costume jewelry.

AN INCOMPLETE GUIDE TO SOME OTHER BERRIES

Mulberries
I am quite crazy about these luscious, fragile fruits. Too soft to send to market in quantity, they are a delicacy among berries, and lucky are those who live within picking distance of a mulberry tree. The fruits—purple-crimson in Europe and red in the American variety—hide behind the tree's large leaves, then drop in brilliant splodges all around the roots. Eat them for what they are, a truly rare treat, with a small amount of cream.

Blueberries *see also page 111*
A beautiful dusty-blue color, and round with a slightly flattened top and bottom, blueberries are perfect for the short-of-time, as there is no need to de-stem or hull. Interesting enough when raw, their flavor is both sharp and bland, but sensational when cooked. One of the world's great berries.

Bilberries
A rare treat found growing wild in Scotland and northern England. Bilberries occasionally make the markets but the somewhat similar tasting blueberry has stolen much of their glory. Smooth skinned and purply-black in color.

Red currants and White currants *see also page 176*
A favorite fruit of mine—it is their acidity that appeals. Generally around during June, July, and August, they are very much a sign that high summer has arrived. Apart from their tartness, which no doubt puts off those for whom sweetness is all, they are annoying to prepare. Having picked them for pocket money as a child I learned to strip them from their delicate stems in seconds. Just hold each sprig in one hand and quickly pull at the diminutive, jewel-like berries using all the fingers of your free hand. Picking each fruit individually will take an age.

Black currants *see also pages 98, 125*
The point of the black currant is the sublime, deeply colored and flavored juices that appear when it is cooked. Apply a little heat and each round, black sphere splits its skin to reveal rich purple juices of great intensity. Only the brave will fail to add sugar, generally 2 heaped tablespoons to the half-pound of berries. A wonderfully strident flavor to perk up crisps, ices, and poached pears. Commercially they are used to produce *crème de cassis*, the purple liqueur which forms the heart of a Kir.

Tayberries
A cross between a raspberry and a blackberry, though the flavor is distinctly more like the latter. Somehow less exciting than its parents, the tayberry is juicy enough to eat on its own with just a little cream.

Fraises des bois **or Alpine Strawberries** *see also pages 55, 178*
The tiniest of the berries, but with a pure flavor reminiscent of a cross between a modern strawberry and vanilla. Its copious little seeds provide a welcome crunchiness that has virtually been bred out of the larger strawberries. I see them rarely in anything but the most elite of markets, and at odd times of the

year, depending on where they are grown. The best, of course, are those you find in the wild, twinkling in the hedgerows like little red and white stars.

Loganberries *see also page 165*
This longer, softer version of the raspberry is a successful result of a blackberry/raspberry cross. First found in California, it has all the joys of a raspberry with the benefit of a little more acidity. Expect to find them in the markets during July and August.

Boysenberries
One of the earliest of the berry family, appearing in early summer, these taste like a tart blackberry. Something of a hybrid experiment, the boysenberry has a parentage of raspberries, blackberries, and loganberries.

CHEAT'S SUMMER PUDDING

Proper English summer pudding should be weighted and left overnight for the juices from the raspberries and red and black currants to soak through the bread. But the different flavors of the berries have already been married in the cooking pot and anyone can soak bread in purple-black juice. So here is a quick version that has much the same flavor, and the same soggy, fruity bread. The only count it fails on is that it just won't stand up. So? Serve it from the bowl, with cream.

FOR 4

6 ounces black currants (1½ cups)	*6 tablespoons sugar*
6 ounces red currants (1½ cups)	*4 slices of white bread*
6 ounces raspberries (1½ cups)	

Remove the stems from the currants. Put the fruit and sugar in a stainless-steel saucepan with 3 tablespoons of water. Bring to a boil, then cook gently till the currants burst their skins and form a rich, purple-red syrup. This usually takes about 5-7 minutes.

Cut the crusts from the bread and cut it in small triangles, about four from each slice. Place a few of them in the bottom of a 9-inch shallow china dish and cover with some of the warm fruit. Make another layer of bread and another of fruit. Continue till all the bread and fruit are used up. It would be a good idea to finish with a layer of bread if you can. Spoon the warm juice over the bread, pressing down gently with the back of a spoon until the bread is completely soaked.

Set aside for as much time as you have. Fifteen minutes should do it. Don't attempt to unmold it from the dish. Spoon into bowls and eat with cream.

BERRIES IN BEAUMES DE VENISE

FOR 4

1 pound blueberries, raspberries, and strawberries

½ bottle of Beaumes de Venise, chilled

Put the berries, cut in half if large, into wineglasses. Fill with the cold Beaumes de Venise and serve immediately.

WARM RED-FRUIT COMPOTE

A ten-minute hot dessert, unless the currants have their stems on, in which case it will take a little longer. Serve with a pitcher of cream, to swirl into the glorious purple-red juices.

FOR 4

½ pound red currants (2 cups)
4 ounces black currants (1 cup)
⅓ cup sugar

1 pound raspberries, loganberries, or tayberries (4 cups)

Put the currants, having first removed their stems, into a stainless-steel saucepan with 2 tablespoons of water and the sugar. Bring slowly to a boil. When the currants start to burst and flood the pan with color, tip in the raspberries, loganberries, or whatever. Simmer for 2 minutes, no longer, and serve them warm, in a white china dish.

RED AND WHITE CURRANTS WITH *FROMAGE BLANC*

Either of the currants is very enjoyable eaten in this way. Unmold some *fromage blanc* onto a plate. Surround it with little sprigs of currants, red and white. Sit in the shade, spreading the fresh, white cheese onto tiny, crisp water biscuits, then scatter over a few red or white currants. Utter bliss.

SIX USES FOR A RED-FRUIT COMPOTE

➤ Serve the compote warm, with store-bought meringues or macaroons and whipped cream

➤ Use the compote as an accompaniment for a sponge cake. Buy a good one from a bakery, and spoon a little compote around each slice

➤ Pour the hot fruit and their juices over vanilla ice cream, watching the ice cream melt into the hot purple syrup

➤ Stir some of the juices into a tub of thick plain yogurt. Eat it straight from the tub

➤ Stir the compote into a bowl of stewed apples

➤ Use the fruit as the filling for crêpes (see page 101), then spoon the juices around the plate

Gooseberries *see also page 62*
I suspect that gooseberries fall into the same category as liver, rhubarb, kidneys, and mackerel. There are those who love them and those who cannot stand them, but few who have no strong feelings either way. For the record, I rank them as one of the finest fruits we grow. I would rather have a bowl of hot baked gooseberries with cold, sharp *crème fraîche* than a bowl of strawberries and cream any day.

I have known some to make more fuss about "topping-and-tailing" gooseberries than is really justified. It takes barely two minutes to de-stem and -flower a pound of goosegogs—I have timed it. Unless the flowers are very large and the stem singularly tough, I am not so sure they always need it anyway. Whatever, you can have them rinsed and prepared in less than five minutes. And they take barely fifteen to cook.

Broiled Gooseberries with Saffron and Honey

Cream and gooseberries is a marriage made in heaven. In this alternative summer dessert the gooseberries are served hot with cold cream or *crème fraîche*, which mingles with the buttery honey and saffron-scented gooseberry juices.

FOR 2

1 pound gooseberries   *pinch of saffron stamens*
butter   *sugar*
2 tablespoons liquid honey   *cream or* crème fraîche, *to serve*

Rinse the fruit in a colander, then top and tail them. Butter an 8-inch baking dish. Be generous. Throw in the goosegogs, the honey, and saffron and stir. Place in a preheated 350°F oven and bake for 15 minutes till they are plump and about to burst.

Remove the dish from the oven and turn on the broiler. Sprinkle with sugar, then broil till caramelized and golden on top. Serve warm, with cream or *crème fraîche*, making the most of the cooking juices.

White Currants in Muscatel

A sparkling Muscatel is, to my mind, a frivolous, light, slightly fizzy wine perfectly suited to drinking out of doors.

A favorite dessert of mine last summer involved a handful of glistening white currants dropped unceremoniously into a wine-glass and topped up with chilled sparkling Muscatel.

Red Currants and Sauternes

Pick the scarlet currants from their fragile stems. Pile them into a glass bowl and sprinkle with sugar and a little very golden, very sweet Sauternes.

PEACHES *see also pages 171, 172, 179*

The perfect fast dessert—a plate of magnificently ripe, crimson-blushed peaches, fragrant from a foot away and wonderfully juicy to eat. This is quite possible to achieve almost year round: I have found peaches in perfect condition from May to October and much more easily than was the case a few years ago.

Even the white peach, once so difficult to find, now makes more than a fleeting appearance in chic supermarkets. Its flesh is creamy-white tinged with vermilion, its scent (to this nose anyway) a cross between roses and raspberries.

A ripe peach is a perfumed one. To test for ripeness, sniff rather than squeeze. The aroma should be sweet. Only the very ripest will require a refrigerator, and will be difficult to get home unbruised. Perhaps better to buy half a dozen at once and ripen them yourself over a few days, in a brown paper bag. Bring them to room temperature before you eat, though, as it is then that their fragrance is at its height.

The peach is the perfect partner for almonds and anything made from them, thick creams with a bite to them, and soft cheeses, even blue ones. Dropped into a glass of not too sweet, very cold wine, it makes one of the best fast desserts I know of.

Nectarines do not hold the same magic for me. I miss the fuzzy skin of the peach, and rarely find the nectarine, its bald cousin, as sexy to eat. But many prefer the nectarine whose scarlet skin is so tempting, and the fruits are, of course, quite interchangeable in the ideas that follow. Late June, July, and August are the best months for these fruits, and their abundance and reasonable price allow one to exploit their juice and flavor all summer long.

STRIPY CHEESE AND BLUSHING FRUIT

There is a chic hybrid cheese that is made up of layers of Dolcelatte and mascarpone, the Italian blue and soft creamy cheeses. It looks too snazzy to be good. In a narrow-minded, elitist sort of way, I ignored it for some time. (I lost out on years of peanut butter and jelly sandwiches that way too.)

I have become very fond of splitting ripe peaches in half, removing the pits, and then stuffing the hollows with blobs of this striped cheese. It is especially good if the cheese is colder than you would usually serve it, and if the peaches are lusciously, dribblingly ripe.

PEACHES WITH ORANGE-BLOSSOM HONEY

You can enlist any of the flower honeys; a mixed one will do fine, but use lavender or orange blossom if you can. Their character seems to come out when warmed under the broiler.

FOR 4

4 tablespoons liquid honey
juice of 1 lemon

2 ripe peaches
4 teaspoons butter

Mix the honey with the lemon juice in a small bowl. Cut the peaches in half and remove the pits. Place the fruit, flat-side up, in a shallow baking dish.

Dot a teaspoon of butter in the hollow of each peach, spoon the lemon and honey mixture over the fruit and place under a preheated broiler, about 5-6 inches from the heat. The peaches are done when the honey starts to bubble and they turn golden brown in patches, about 5-7 minutes.

Amaretti Peaches

Follow the previous recipe, but forget the butter. Before you spoon the honey and lemon over, stuff the peach halves with the following mixture:

FOR 4

¼ cup ricotta cheese
6 amaretti cookies, crushed in their papers
   or in a paper bag with a rolling pin

Spoon the honey and lemon over and place under the pre-heated broiler until the almond-cheese filling begins to brown, about 5-7 minutes. Serve hot, spooning the syrup from the baking dish over the peaches.

Poached Peaches with Grand Marnier

FOR 2

4 ripe peaches, not too large	*1 vanilla bean*
½ cup sugar	*4 slices of orange*
1 cup water	*2 tablespoons Grand Marnier*

Halve the peaches and remove the pits. Put the sugar, water, vanilla, and orange slices, but not the liqueur, in a pan large enough to hold the fruit in one layer. Bring to a boil and turn down to a simmer. Add the fruit and poach it gently. The syrup should just cover the peaches; if it doesn't then make a little more.

After 5-10 minutes the peaches, depending on their ripeness, will be tender and soaked with the vanilla and orange syrup. Remove from the heat. Place the peaches in a serving dish, then spoon the syrup over. Add the Grand Marnier and leave to cool a little before eating.

Peach Melba

People scoff at peach Melbas. And well they might—there is something deeply unchic about such things. But a peach Melba can be a thing of joy. If you can excuse its garish orange, pink, and white, it can taste quite superb. But there are rules.

➤ The peach must be ripe. It must never have seen a can

➤ The peach should be poached lightly in vanilla-scented syrup

➤ The sauce should be made from puréed raspberries. There is no reason why they couldn't have been frozen at some point

➤ The ice cream should be vanilla, not Neapolitan, and should be of the very best quality

➤ It should really be called *Pêches Melba*

FOR 4

4 ripe peaches	*½ pound raspberries (2 cups)*
2 heaped tablespoons sugar	*very good vanilla ice cream*
1 vanilla bean	

Place the whole peaches in a saucepan with just enough water to cover them. Throw in the sugar and the vanilla bean. Bring to a boil and poach them in simmering water for 8-10 minutes. Remove with a slotted spoon. The peaches are ready when their skins peel off easily. Do this carefully so as not to damage the fruit. Cut each one in half and gently ease out the pit. Place the peach halves in a cool place.

Get four glass bowls as cold as you can. Whizz the raspberries in the food processor until they are puréed (you can strain them at this point to remove the seeds if you wish). Taste the purée. You may feel it needs a little sugar. I can't honestly say I have ever added any to a raspberry purée, but if you want a sweeter result now is the time to get the confectioners' sugar out.

Place a large, solid ball of ice cream in each chilled dish. Place one half of peach on each side of the ice cream, then drizzle the raspberry purée over.

The Cream Question

There are some who say that a peach Melba is not a peach Melba unless it has whipped cream on it. No doubt that is what old Escoffier, the Savoy's chef, meant when he produced the dessert to honor Dame Nellie Melba. I insist that it is better without. But you may well disagree. Add a dollop of cream if you wish, whipped quite stiff with a little vanilla extract.

But then if you are going to add a swirl of whipped cream, you might as well stick a maraschino cherry on top, too.

MARZIPAN PEACHES

Heat the broiler. Cut ripe peaches in half and remove the pits. Put a lump of almond paste in the hollow of each peach half. Sprinkle with rosewater and broil till the almond paste melts and turns golden, about 7-8 minutes. Eat warm.

HOT PEACHES WITH MASCARPONE AND PINE NUTS

FOR 2

4 ripe peaches
4 heaped tablespoons
   mascarpone cheese

2 heaped tablespoons pine nuts

Cut the peaches in half and remove the pits. Put the peaches in a shallow ovenproof dish, flat-side up. Dot half a tablespoon of mascarpone in the hollow of each peach. Scatter pine nuts over the cheese and place under a preheated broiler till the cheese has melted and the pine nuts are golden.

PEACHES WITH BRIOCHE

My local supermarket has started selling rather good brioche. It is a little "cakey," but then Islington isn't Paris. I like eating the rich, yellow bread with a whole ripe peach. It is more of a snack than a dessert, but the two match up quite well, like figs and *ciabatta*.

Peaches with Raspberry Sauce

Pour boiling water over ripe peaches. Leave for 5 minutes, then carefully remove them from the water. Peel away the skins; they should lift off easily. Put a whole peach in the center of each plate.

Whizz raspberries, fresh or frozen ones, in the blender or food processor with a few drops of Kirsch or some other compatible alcohol, and reduce to a purée. I think you had better strain it to remove the little seeds. You might add a little lemon juice if you think about it. Pour the purée around the peaches and serve slightly chilled. The ubiquitous mint leaf, so beloved of young chefs, would actually serve some purpose here, though it would be better chopped up and scattered over the dish.

You will probably need to eat this with a fork and a spoon. Otherwise the peach is likely to go slithering off the plate like a bar of wet soap.

Peaches with Port

I learned to like port wine on a fact-finding trip to Portugal. My hosts were one of the old port families whose *quintas* line the banks of the Douro, and I was plied with the stuff for my entire stay. (And for a good while afterwards.) It was the light white port that got to me; mixed with tonic and mint leaves it made a very pleasant early-evening drink by the pool. After a little while the bottles started to mount up and, when the weather turned cooler, I started using it in other ways. This was by far the most successful, and I think worth repeating.

FOR 2

2 peaches, ripe and juicy   *a little sugar*
2 tablespoons white port wine

Slice the peaches into a bowl. Discard the pits. Sprinkle the port over them, then a little sugar. You might like the taste of the peaches without any sweetener, so try them first. Set aside for 20 minutes.

A Plate of White Peaches and Red Berries

A dessert plate for the end of a high-summer meal. Arrange heavily perfumed white peaches on a pretty plate with a handful of fresh almonds, shelled but not skinned, and a little pile of deep red loganberries or raspberries.

Hot Peaches with Red-Currant Jelly

I suggest you buy some decent red-currant jelly for this, so that the sauce tastes of fruit rather than sugar. Some of the French brands are good.

FOR 2
1 cup red-currant jelly
4 ripe peaches

Melt the jelly in a small saucepan; if it is a good brand it won't be too thick, but you may need to add a little water to achieve a smooth, slightly runny sauce. Cut the peaches in half, remove the pits and warm the peaches in the red-currant sauce. Serve warm.

➤ Rose-petal jam, from Middle-Eastern grocers or posh food emporiums, is delightful used in this way

➤ So is quince jam, if you can find a brand that is quite soft and melts easily. Some of them are quite stiff

➤ If there is any leftover, it will be just as good tomorrow, especially if left in the cool rather than in the refrigerator

APRICOTS *see also page 60*

Apricots have a subtle, annoyingly elusive flavor and a fluffy texture. I am sure this is not how they should be. But it is increasingly how I find them. Lucky people who have eaten them straight from the tree assure me that they have a blushing, peach-like flesh and, when perfectly ripe, are blessed with a deep, sweet flavor.

I buy them, hoping each time they will be as good as I gather they can be. But I am invariably disappointed. I will not assume that you have any more luck when shopping than I do. The few ideas here are not for fools and mousses where the elusive flavor is smothered with bland ingredients, but instead the fruit is matched with something that teases out its shy flavor: sharp creams, sweet muscat wines, aniseedy fennel, and, in one case, the application of a little heat and sugar.

BROILED APRICOTS WITH MASCARPONE

Golden apricots with a glistening sugary top.

FOR 2

6 ripe apricots
12 heaped teaspoons (3 ounces)
   mascarpone cheese

⅓ cup sugar

Heat the broiler. Halve and pit the apricots and put them, hollow-side up, in a heatproof dish. Place a spoonful of mascarpone in each hollow. Sprinkle with half of the sugar and place the dish under the broiler, close to the heat. Cook for 4 minutes, then remove from the heat, and sprinkle the remaining sugar over. Broil once more, till the fruit is tender with a crisp crust. Eat warm.

➤ Peaches work in this recipe too, as of course do nectarines. And I have also had success with dark red plums

Apricots Stuffed with Ricotta and Fennel

Apricots respond to any piquant cheese or cream. I perk up the overly subtle flavor of apricots with *crème fraîche*, thick yogurt, and, increasingly, ricotta cheese. Sometimes I mix them; ricotta or cottage cheese with yogurt is a favorite. Surprisingly, some of the blue cheeses, such as salty and expensive Roquefort or less salty and less expensive gorgonzola, make instant stuffings for apricots or peaches.

FOR 4

12 ripe apricots
½ cup ricotta cheese
⅔ cup thick plain yogurt

2 tablespoons chopped herb
fennel and its fronds

Cut the apricots in half just enough to pull out the pit. Try to keep the fruit intact at one point, which is easy enough to do if you follow the natural split in the fruit with your thumb. Set the fruit down on a plate. Mix the cheese and yogurt, then stir in the fennel.

Spoon the fennel-cheese mixture into the open apricots. A little sprig of green fennel frond in each fruit would be a nice touch if you can be bothered.

Apricots with Beaumes de Venise

Useful stuff, this sticky wine. The muscat tones of Beaumes de Venise are one way of making apricots laugh a little louder. Slice the ripe fruit, quarters will do, and drop the pieces into glasses of the chilled, sweet golden wine.

Apricots with Strawberry and Orange Sauce

Cut several ripe apricots in half. Remove the pits and place the fruit in a dish large enough to take them in a single layer. Butt them up closely with their hollows facing up. Whizz ripe strawberries in the food processor, and add the juice of an orange and a little of its grated zest. Spoon the purée over the fruit. Leave for a little while before serving.

Warm Apricot Tarts

Crisp thin pastry. Juicy fruit.

FOR 2, GENEROUSLY

½ pound puff pastry *8 ripe apricots*
(thawed if frozen) *sugar*

Roll out the pastry to a thickness of ⅛ inch, which is thinner than you would normally expect. Cut two 6-inch disks of pastry and place on a baking sheet or wooden board. Chill for 15 minutes.

Preheat the oven to 425°F. Place an empty baking sheet in the oven. Place the apricots in a heatproof bowl and cover with boiling water. Leave for 1 minute, then remove with a slotted spoon.

Cut the apricots in half, peeling away the downy skin as you go. Remove the pits. Place the apricot halves, flat-side down, on the chilled pastry disks and dust with a little sugar.

Transfer each one, using a pancake turner or some such implement, to the hot baking sheet. The heat will help the pastry to crisp nicely. Bake for 10 minutes until puffed, crisp, and golden. Eat while warm.

The *Brûlée*

Fruit, cream, and sugar are combined in this glorious dessert, which no matter how extravagant its ingredients and indulgent its nature remains eternally popular. Its popularity rests no doubt on the mixture of textures between ripe fruit, thick, rich cream, and crackling caramel crust.

In essence easy, the method is actually beset with little pitfalls, which can leave you with a sloppy mess resembling fruit soup.

The Cream

A stiff *crème fraîche* is my first choice, as it has something to offer in the way of flavor as well as voluptuousness. A sharp heavy cream would be my second. The cream should have flavor to it; a good-quality heavy cream has more point to it than sheer unctuousness. Flat-tasting ultra-pasteurized creams provide creaminess but little else. Whipping cream, because of its lower butterfat content, tends to "fall" when the boiling caramel is poured over, and weeps if left for more than a few minutes before eating. Yogurt is more successful than you might think, though it is prone to tantrums. Occasionally it curdles horribly when under the broiler or when it meets the hot caramel, but generally can be relied upon if it is thick and cold enough.

The Fruit
It is essential that the chosen fruit is compatible with cream and sugar. Too often I have encountered *brûlées* consisting of inappropriate fruits such as apples, underripe pears, and oranges. While these fruits are accessible and cheap, they are, I think, better used in other ways. No, *brûlées* only work when the fruit is right. Something a little tart that will shine through the cream and sugar is vital; for me this could be raspberries, black-berries, or very lightly cooked blueberries. Something juicy such as peaches or nectarines is welcome, and the colors are appealing. To my mind, bananas are pretty much unbeatable for providing reasonably priced bulk and an affinity with thick cream.

Grapes are fine, as they enjoy being covered in caramel, and burst unexpectedly in the mouth as you eat. Red currants and pineapples are other tangy additions that serve a purpose. If the fruits are sweet, that is very ripe strawberries, mango, and banana, the dish will cloy. If it is to be good it needs a little bite.

The Sugar
Fine granulated sugar works best for both pot-made caramel and for broiling. It is important that the sugar is "clean," in other words, there are no bits of flour or butter in there, or, heaven forbid, the lumps that appear when someone else has dipped in a wet coffee spoon.

Making the Caramel
Pot method I prefer this method for making a large *brûlée*. Put the sugar into a heavy-based, deep saucepan. Thin pans are almost always pitted or warped and develop hot spots that allow the sugar to cook unevenly, burning in patches and not even

melting in others. A deepish pan is essential; I once scalded myself quite badly using too shallow a pan, the hot caramel swooshing up over the edge when I grabbed it too quickly from the heat.

Incidentally, I can never get the caramel to work properly in a nonstick pan. It is also nigh impossible to see the changing color of the caramel as it turns from shining golden caramel to throat-rasping, thick black smoke.

Pour just enough water into the pan to wet the sugar through. You can, of course, put in more, but as it has to evaporate anyway there seems little point. Put the pan over medium-high heat, otherwise it will take forever. Leave the pan alone, and do not stir the mixture. If it looks as if the mixture is cooking unevenly, then move the sugar gently around the pan with a clean long-handled spoon.

When the sugar starts to turn golden, after anything from 4 to 15 minutes, you must keep a very close watch over it. When it becomes golden you can move the pan from side to side to encourage even coloring, but by no means stir it. When it is golden brown, but before it starts to smoke, lift it from the heat and (remembering it is blisteringly hot) pour it quickly over the cream. It will set to a crisp in parts while causing rivulets of molten cream and caramel to run down in others.

Broiler method Heat the broiler in advance, and get it as hot as you can. The idea is to caramelize the sugar without allowing the heat to penetrate the cream or yogurt. Sprinkle a thin layer of absolutely clean sugar on top of the cream and fruit. It should be as thick as a half-dollar. The cream should be as cold as you can get it. Place under the hot broiler, close to the heat, until the sugar has melted and turned golden. Unless you have a professional-style broiler it is likely that the sugar will caramelize unevenly, so turn the dish around to get an even tan. Invariably, this method produces a more liquid result.

The worst thing that can go wrong with either method is that a) you will burn yourself or b) you will undercook the caramel, turning it sticky, or overcook it, turning it bitter. Once *brûléed*, the dish should not be refrigerated.

Banana, Peach, and Raspberry *Brûlée*

¾ cup sugar
1½ pounds mixed bananas,
  peaches, and raspberries

1½ cups chilled heavy
  cream

Read the instructions on page 168 first. Put the sugar in a heavy pan and pour in enough water to cover. Set over medium-high heat to boil, while you prepare the fruit. Peel the bananas; pit and slice the peaches; and remove any stems from the raspberries. Put all the fruit in a heatproof serving bowl. Although it looks wonderful in a shining cut bowl, remember that it is not the easiest thing in the world to scrape encrusted caramel from a fragile glass dish.

Whip the cream until it forms stiff peaks. If it starts to look grainy then you have overwhipped it. Spoon the cream in high waves over the fruit.

The sugar in the saucepan will start to turn a pale golden caramel after 10 minutes—watch it carefully as it is prone to burning. The caramel is ready when it turns a *rich* golden brown. Immediately, taking care not to splash or burn yourself, pour the caramel over the cream and fruit. It will at once set to a crisp, shiny coat. Eat within 30 minutes.

A *Brûlée* of Scarlet Fruits

¾ cup sugar
1½ pounds assorted red fruits:
  raspberries, strawberries, red
  currants, blackberries,
  loganberries, etc.

1½ cups crème fraîche
  (or heavy cream, whipped
  to soft peaks)

Follow the instructions on page 168, but do not try to whip the *crème fraîche*. Instead, spoon the cream over the fruit, making peaks as best you can. Lay a few sprigs of red currants or little piles of berries over the peaks and then pour over the golden caramel.

OTHER COMBINATIONS TO TRY UNDER THE CREAM AND SUGAR

➤ Peaches, pineapples, and mangoes

➤ Bananas, figs, blackberries, and black grapes

➤ Bananas, strawberries, and blueberries (the blueberries cooked briefly with a little sugar and a spoon of water till they just burst)

➤ Watermelon chunks, blackberries, and nectarine

➤ Apricots, plums, and blackberries

NECTARINE-YOGURT BURNT CREAM

Burnt cream is just another name for a *brûlée*. Read the note on page 168 first.

You will need those sweet little white china ramekins or a shallow dish similar to a quiche dish for this. Two-thirds fill the dishes with pitted and chopped nectarines, though you could use peaches if that is what you have. Cover the fruit with thick plain yogurt (drained of excess liquid) and smooth flat with the blade of a knife. Sprinkle with sugar, making sure you completely cover the yogurt to the thickness of a half-dollar. Place on the broiler pan and cook under a preheated hot broiler till the sugar starts to caramelize, probably a couple of minutes. You may have to turn the dishes around to achieve an even effect.

➤ You need not stick to nectarines or even peaches. Use any ripe fruit compatible with yogurt; try ban~   ~rries, or raspberries for a start

MELONS

One of the greatest joys of shopping in France is being able to sort through the melons piled high on street market trestle tables, picking them up and weighing them in the hand to find the heaviest for its size, and sniffing deeply to ascertain ripeness. This is heaven. I can just imagine trying to pick out the best fruit in my local street market in North London. I would probably be frogmarched down the road. And then street traders wonder why we shop at the big-name supermarkets.

Melon suffered from its social position in Britain as one of three appetizers offered in steak houses (the others being soup of the day and shrimp cocktail). The melon was invariably Honeydew, not exactly the most delectable variety, and was usually unripe: how to give a fruit a bad name.

A ripe melon, at its finest moment, is hard to improve upon. If the point of eating a fruit is its fragrance, flavor, and sweet juice, then you cannot do better than a Charentais or Canteloupe melon (I am talking here of the true Canteloupe, although what Americans call Cantaloupe—actually a muskmelon—is also very sweet and juicy). I can think of no other fruit which, when perfect, can give such pleasure, unless, perhaps, you are picking mulberries from the tree.

Look for melons that weigh heavily and, probably, have a strong aroma, though that can be an unreliable guide as some keep their smell to themselves until cut. They should be tender, perhaps even a little soft at the stem end, though they require only a gentle squeeze to assure; prodding and poking will only damage the fruit. (I once witnessed a man in a supermarket squirt himself with a fountain of juice after being less than gentle with a Galia.)

A SOMEWHAT INCOMPLETE GUIDE TO MELON VARIETIES

Canteloupe
This popular European melon has a long season from late summer till almost Christmas. The rough, one could say scabby, greeny-yellow skin hides an orange or green flesh with a wonderful flavor. To my mind not as magnificent as the Charentais, I think it is at its best served with slightly salty accompaniments such as prosciutto or olives. The American "Cantaloupe" has a raised netting on its skin, and the sweet, fragrant flesh is pale orange.

Ogen

Ogen melons appear in midsummer and last through till late autumn. They have a green flesh beneath round yellow- and green-sectioned skin. Not my favorite variety, as they can sometimes be really quite watery.

Watermelon

Summer wouldn't be the same without watermelons, which are in season from July to October. These huge, dark green cannonballs or torpedos can be too much of a good thing. It may be wiser to buy a half or quarter. The color of the flesh varies from soft pink to bright crimson, though this is not necessarily a sign of ripeness. Flavor is not really the point here, though there can be few things I enjoy more than biting into a huge red melon slice, chilled to the point of freezing, on a roastingly hot summer's day.

Honeydew

Cheap and cheerful, sometimes a boring eat, but better than no melon at all. Recognized by its football shape, rock-hard yellow skin, and watery, pale green flesh. Its juice, though copious when ripe, is hardly the most luscious. A refreshing fruit, though, and fine for tossing with strawberries and blackberries for a summer salad. It is pretty much available all year.

Cranshaw

A wonderful, fragrant, juicy melon, with a sweet aroma.

Charentais

My favorite melon is the Charentais, certainly the smallest of the melons, but to my mind the finest of them all. This delectable fruit is with us from July to September only and is easily recognized by its round shape, deep segmenting, and soft jade-green color. The flesh inside is a revelation: salmony-orange in color and deeply, deeply fragrant. Cut them carefully so as not to lose any of their juices, and eat them lightly chilled. Do nothing, absolutely nothing, to a perfect specimen. Enjoy its scented flesh for what it is—possibly the finest fruit there is.

A *MÉLANGE* OF MELONS

At a summer's lunch in the sunshine it would be difficult to find anything more welcome than a plate of ripe, smiling melon slices for dessert. Find your biggest plate, an oval platter, if you have one. Cover it with slices cut from as many different melons as you can lay your hands on: creamy-yellow Honeydew; pale salmon-pink Charentais; green Galia; and, of course, scarlet watermelon. Arrange them in an impromptu fashion rather than following any scheme, and serve them thoroughly chilled.

MELON WITH RASPBERRIES AND *FRAMBOISE*

FOR 2

1 ripe, medium melon	*1 heaped tablespoon sugar*
1 tablespoon framboise	*¾ pound raspberries (3 cups)*

Cut the stem end from the melon about 1 inch or so from the top. This will form a lid. You can cut it in a zigzag pattern if it pleases you, though I can't say it is something I would do myself. Scoop out the seeds and discard.

With a metal spoon scrape out the flesh, keeping the pieces as large as possible, or you can use a melon baller if you have one. Try not to tear the melon skin, which is to act as a serving dish. Cut the melon pieces in chunks and put them into a bowl with the *framboise* and sugar. Stir gently. Spoon the melon and its juices back into the melon shell, then stir in the raspberries gently, so as not to break them up.

Chill if you can before eating. It really does look, taste, and smell wonderful. Put it in the center of the table and let each person eat it with a spoon.

PARTNERS FOR MELON

Sugar and ground ginger do nothing for a melon other than insult a noble fruit. A little salt, and I do mean a little, will bring out the flavor like nothing else. So will a salty cured ham such as mountain-cured Serrano from Spain or a *prosciutto crudo* from Parma, Italy. I offer the suggestion of cheese with melon to finish a meal, or for a snack in its own right. Feta, the deliciously salty white cheese from Greece, is one, as is a piece of well-aged Parmesan or pecorino. If serving a mixed plate of melon and cheese I would throw in a handful of olives, too.

TOM JAINE'S MELON, RED CURRANTS, AND CASSIS

A recipe from Tom Jaine, from his book *Cooking in the Country*, which is a collection of his newsletters written to regular guests at The Carved Angel restaurant in Dartmouth. I will not argue with Tom's preference for the Charentais variety, despite my earlier comments, though I might suggest that you could use another.

FOR 2

½ cup sugar
6 tablespoons water
¼ cup crème de cassis
1 cup of red currants,
   removed from stems

juice of ½ lemon
1 Charentais melon

Make a syrup of the sugar and water; take off the heat and add the *cassis* and then the red currants. Let this cool fully. Season with the lemon juice. Cut the melon in slices and scoop away the seeds. Peel the slices and cut further into thin chunks. Mix.

Honeydew and White Port Wine

Honeydew needs a little help if it is to be good. Choose a very yellow-skinned melon and cut it roughly in large chunks, discarding the seeds. Each chunk should be large enough to fill a dessert spoon; little pieces look horrid. Sprinkle with chilled white port wine and chopped mint leaves. You will need 3 healthy-looking sprigs of mint and 3 tablespoons of white port per melon. Remember that a little mint goes a long way.

Utter Bliss

Several people lay claim to this recipe. I first came across it when working up in the English Lake District, at John Tovey's Miller Howe to be precise. This was one of the most popular dishes there, though I seem to remember it being served as a first course, which would be very much in the style of the place. This is not quite John Tovey's recipe. Believe the name.

FOR 2

a ripe, medium melon	*1 heaped tablespoon sugar*
4 ounces strawberries	*sparkling wine*
(about 1 cup)	

Cut the melon in half. Scoop out and discard the seeds and stringy bits. Whizz the berries to a purée, and sweeten with a little sugar (this is surprisingly necessary once the sparkling wine goes in). Set the melon in a serving dish so that it will not wobble. You can trim the base a little, but don't make a hole in the melon skin.

Pour the strawberry purée into the hollow, then fill up with sparkling wine. Eat while still sparkling.

CANTELOUPE AND *FRAISES DES BOIS*

Halve the Canteloupe (or muskmelon), scoop out the seeds, losing as little of the juice as you can, and then scatter a few tiny wild strawberries over. I find a tablespoon of berries just enough for half a small Canteloupe. If your fruit is a large one, then cut it in quarters or even sixths, put the slices on a generous-sized plate, and throw over the little berries.

CRANSHAW AND BASIL

Wonderful combination this. Tear up a handful of basil leaves or shred them with a knife, sprinkle the leaves over a small halved and seeded Cranshaw melon, and eat at once while the melon is still chilled and the basil still has its pepperiness.

MELON AND HONEY

A good way to perk up a Honeydew or a Cranshaw melon. Cut the fruit in large pieces, discarding the seeds, of course, and the skin. If you have one of those dinky melon ballers you could use it to great effect here. Drop the fruit into a bowl, drizzle about 2 tablespoons of honey per half melon over the top, and leave for 15 minutes or so before eating. Flower honeys are more suitable here than herb and heather ones, and liquid honey is more successful than set.

MELON AND CHEESE

Not a dessert especially, but worth mentioning all the same, was a snack plate I made for myself one afternoon consisting of chunks of rather dull but juicy Honeydew melon jumbled with thin slices of sharp farmhouse Cheddar. It was really rather good, and was made in five minutes.

Melon, Peaches, and Nectarines with *Amaretto*

Serve the three together in a salad with a sprinkling of the almond liqueur. An idea lifted from the late Jeremy Round's classic, *The Independent Cook*.

Charentais and . . .

No. There is absolutely nothing that will improve a perfectly ripe, luscious Charentais. Take the soft green fruit somewhere quiet (I suggest the garden) and eat it chilled, all by yourself, *sans* sugar, salt, cream, berries, or any other good idea that springs to mind. Any addition would be an intrusion.

Watermelon with Feta

A summer snack or original ending. Cut the watermelon in large chunks, though nothing bigger than you would put in your mouth in one go, and toss the chunks with hunks of feta cheese, broken roughly from the block. Serve cold, with a handful of shredded basil leaves.

Melon with Blackberries

Slightly tart blackberries and ripe green-fleshed melon, Canteloupe or Cranshaw for preference, are a delightful way to end a meal, particularly if it has been quite rich. This combination looks its best when the melon is served in mouth-sized chunks and a few dark berries have been dotted among them in a white bowl.

CHEESES FOR SUMMER

Soft goat cheeses are for many the high spot of the cheese year. Fresh goat's milk cheeses, soft, white, and usually sold in fez-shaped pieces, have an unmatchable piquancy and freshness. Often sold rolled in chopped dill fronds or chives (too many to my mind), these cheeses make a charming finale to a meal. One cheese will serve two with a little bread.

A favorite dessert of mine, if you can extend the term to such an idea, is to put a smooth white goat cheese in the center of a smooth white plate and scatter around it whole strawberries, their leaves intact to hold on to. As I eat, I spread each berry with a generous mouthful of cheese.

Of the cow's milk varieties, Pont l'Evêque, from Normandy, is very much a summer cheese. A good one will be like a plump, square cushion, an amber to soft pumpkin in color with sweet, tangy flesh. What I call a knife and fork cheese, it is best eaten without any accompaniment, even bread.

Other summer cheeses include sweet, earthy, semi-soft mountain Reblochon; salty, tangy, crumbly feta (even the plastic-wrapped stuff is okay, especially when eaten in alternate mouthfuls with fresh raw peas); and white, crumbly ricotta, the Italian fresh cheese. Make sure that the ricotta is brilliant white, crumbly, and moist. Don't buy any that is yellowing—it taints easily, and loses its subtle freshness quicker than most. Equally good, though as different a mouthful as you can get, is an aged Parmesan. A tangy, deeply savory bite, just break off a lump with a short sharp knife and munch it as you clear away the supper things.

ACKNOWLEDGMENTS

Recipes must come from somewhere. They don't just hit you like a bolt from the blue when you are doing the ironing or feeding the cat. For the most part I have acknowledged my sources and inspirations in the text, but there will be omissions. I would like to thank the authors and cooks who have given me permission to use their recipes and quotes and, in particular, those whose good ideas I have mercilessly exploited to my own ends. I am grateful, too, to Fay Maschler for letting me quote from her column in the *Evening Standard*, to Sophie Grigson for allowing me to use her words from the *Independent*, and to Lynda Brown for her advice and inspiration.

Once again my thanks to Louise Haines, my editor at Michael Joseph, for her patience and for turning a chaotic manuscript into a readable book. My thanks, too, to Christabel Gairdner. I am indebted to illustrator and author Val Archer, whose beautiful drawings have so accurately captured the spirit of the text, and once again to Kevin Summers for his photographs. And to Nancy Roberts, my editor at *marie claire*, for her patience and continuing support.

BIBLIOGRAPHY

Battiscombe, Georgina, *English Picnics*, Harvill Press, 1949

Beard, James, *James Beard's American Cookery*, Little, Brown, 1980

Bissell, Frances, *The Pleasures of Cooking*, Chatto and Windus, 1986

Bissell, Frances, *The Book of Food*, Henry Holt & Co., 1994

Brown, Catherine, *Scottish Cookery*, Richard Drew, 1985

Brown, Lynda, *The Cook's Garden*, Century, 1990

Bunyard, Edward, *The Anatomy of Dessert*, Chatto and Windus, 1933

Child, Julia, *The Way to Cook*, Alfred A. Knopf, 1993

Christian, Glynn, *Glynn Christian's Delicatessen Handbook*, Macdonald, 1982

Costa, Margaret, *The Four Seasons Cookery Book*, Nelson, 1970

Crabtree and Evelyn Cookbook, Stewart Tabori & Chang, 1989

Croft-Cooke, Rupert, *English Cooking*, W. H. Allen, 1960

David, Elizabeth, *Elizabeth David Classics: Mediterranean Food, French Country Cooking, Summer Cooking*, Alfred A. Knopf, 1980

Davidson, Alan and Charlotte Knox, *Fruit*, Mitchell Beazley, 1991

Del Conte, Anna, *Entertaining All'Italiana*, Bantam, 1991

Gavin, Paola, *Italian Vegetarian Cooking*, M. Evans and Co., 1994

Graham, Peter, *Classic Cheese Cookery*, Penguin, 1988

Gray, Patience, *Honey from a Weed*, Prospect Books, 1986

Grigson, Jane, *Good Things*, Michael Joseph, 1971

Grigson, Jane, *Jane Grigson's Fruit Book*, Michael Joseph, 1982

Grigson, Sophie, *Gourmet Ingredients*, Van Nostrand Reinhold, 1991

Hambro, Natalie, *Visual Delights*, Little, Brown, 1986

Hazan, Marcella, *Classic Italian Cookbook*, Macmillan, 1980

Heath, Ambrose, *Good Savouries*, Faber & Faber, 1939

Hegarty, Patricia, *An English Flavour*, Equation, 1988

Holt, Geraldene, *Geraldene Holt's Complete Book of Herbs*, Conran Octopus, 1991

Jaine, Tom, *Cooking in the Country*, Chatto and Windus, 1986

Lassalle, George, *George Lassalle's Middle Eastern Food East of Orphanides*, Trafalgar, 1993

Madison, Deborah, *Greens Cookbook*, Bantam, 1988

Maschler, Fay, *Eating In*, Bloomsbury, 1987

Molyneaux, Joyce and Sophie Grigson, *The Carved Angel Cookery Book*, Harper Collins, 1994

Nicholson, B. E., *Oxford Book of Food Plants*, Oxford University Press, 1969

Pomaine, Edouard de, *Cooking In Ten Minutes*, Cookery Book Club, 1969

Rance, Patrick, *The Great British Cheese Book*, Macmillan, 1983

Roden, Claudia, *A New Book of Middle Eastern Food*, Viking, 1985

Round, Jeremy, *The Independent Cook*, Barrie and Jenkins, 1985

Shere, Lindsey R. *Chez Panisse Desserts*, Random House, 1985

Slater, Nigel, *Real Fast Food*, The Overlook Press, 1996

Slater, Nigel, *The marie claire Cook Book*, Paul Hamlyn, 1992

Smith, Delia, *Delia Smith's Complete Cookery Course*, BBC Books, 1978

Smith, Michael, *The Afternoon Tea Book*, Simon & Schuster, 1989

Stobart, Tom, *Spices, Herbs and Flavorings*, The Overlook Press, 1986

Toklas, Alice B., *The Alice B. Toklas Cookbook*, Harper Collins, 1986

Waters, Alice, *Chez Panisse Menu Cookbook*, Random House, 1982

INDEX